MW01279874

Printed in the United States of America.

tsingleton@sscoachingsolutions.com
https://sscoachingsolutions.com
https://TalkWithTrevor.com

Editing: www.WritersWay.com
Cover: Momentum Graphix & Copy, LLC
Published by: Single Source Coaching Solutions, LLC

ISBN: 979-8-9883906-1-9

Disclaimer

The purpose of this book is to educate and empower. The author does not guarantee that anyone following these techniques, suggestions, tips, ideas, or strategies will achieve a particular result. The author shall have neither liability nor responsibility with respect to any loss or damage caused, or alleged to be caused, directly or indirectly by the information contained in this book.

To my wife, Nicole. I love you dearly and look forward to more great times with you. Though we've been married for years, this is just the beginning.

CONTENTS

Introduction

Old keys won't open new doors.

I've been a student of self-improvement and leadership training since I can remember. School was fun for me, though less educational. I mostly enjoyed the social aspect of it. Being able to hang with my friends, having pencil fights (I'm dating myself a bit), having fun at recess, talking about the latest music. To me, the learning depended on the teacher and the atmosphere that was set. I could learn in a class, but I understood better on my own. Reading books, using my imagination—those were activities I liked. I remember spending hours at the library reading mystery novels, comic books, and stories of adventure. It was perfect for an only child like me, to be able to get lost in those adventures and escape the loneliness that surrounded me.

One of the first books I recall buying was John Maxwell's *The 21 Irrefutable Laws of Leadership*. I was already a fan of books, but this was on another level. It was the first book I saw that had a count of something: 21 laws. He followed that up with *The 21 Indispensable Qualities of a Leader* and *The 21 Most Powerful Minutes in a Leader's Day*. These books appealed to me because I'm into numbers. I was born on December 31. My mom is a tax accountant, so I always joke that I was Mommy's tax deduction. She had impeccable timing.

I also became intrigued with the number 3, especially when I found out that you can add up a large number, and if the total is divisible by 3, then the number is as well. So, 21 laws made sense to me. John Maxwell knew he'd hit onto something. His subsequent books also had numbers in the titles. I became a committed fan and bought all his books.

However, another game changer was waiting in the wings for me: a book called *Learn How to Use the Other 90%*. I was stunned! What was this? As I started researching, I uncovered the popular medical concept of people only using 10% of their brain. That started me on my journey of self-improvement. Anything that had a cool cover and a great title, especially with a number in it, was a book I had to buy.

If you're paying close attention, you'll notice that I said "bought" not read. I became an avid collector of literary books on self-improvement, leadership, wealth, and business. Most of the books I purchased became "shelf-help" books. Though I had books on businesses and ways to create multiple streams of income, I just collected them. Sometimes I would start reading and underlining, though I never finished them. At one point my book budget diminished, and my buying slowed down. Then I discovered my local library which had an assortment of books on my favorite subjects. I couldn't keep them and underline in them, of course, which I would love to do, just extend my temporary use of them.

I did eventually discover and clarify that I wanted a position where I could help people learn, develop, and discover gifts within themselves. I'd spent over 20 years in positions involving training and development, management, and leadership. Many times, I would take the lead in training new hires. My goal was, and still is, to pass on what I know and make sure people don't bang into the same walls I did. In the back of my mind, though, I'd often thought about starting my own business.

My last position before eventually launching my own business as a coach was again training and development. I had the pleasure of traveling to clients who purchased financial planning software for their companies. Finally, I was in my element, training CFOs, VPs of Finance, Directors, Managers, and key people in an organization who would roll it out to others. My skillset was put to full use training the implementation of the software, as well as fostering conversation that would impact all areas of the company, such as budget, expenses, revenue, and personnel.

Yes, it *was* numbers and yes, it *was* reports. But the best part was showing these leaders something that could not only alleviate hours of painstaking work but give them the opportunity to improve and create new reports for better decision-making.

I got so much pleasure showing the leadership the software, but more importantly, giving them the space to create new reports instead of relying on the old ones. Many people need that verbal permission that it's okay to go into new territory that's been the topic of discussion for years but hasn't made it to fruition. It also didn't hurt that I was a bit of a foodie. Being able to travel to multiple states and try different restaurants I'd seen on TV or read in articles was a great experience. (But that's for another book).

As the pandemic hit in 2020 and travel slowed to halt, I found myself in a position when I could finally start my coaching business. I'd thought about doing that for more than 15 years while I was getting my master's degree. But at that time, coaching seemed to be a saturated field. You couldn't throw a rock without hitting a different type of coach. So, frustration set in, coupled with long standing procrastination, and I found myself in a familiar place: waiting for opportunity to knock on the door.

Sensing my state of mind, my wife sent me a link to purchase a self-paced course on Life Coaching. From there, I created my website and began networking, making connections, and building partnerships. It was a whole new world I had entered. I was finally given the right key to open the right door!

Like many entrepreneurs, I started posting online to various social media platforms. Comments and likes were coming, although no business. I saw the value of using YouTube for marketing my coaching business by putting out videos to increase client awareness. Thus, the creation and formation of the book you're holding, which is a result of the many videos I produced. Numerous titles have come to me in the past, but this book is the doorway for me to begin my journey as an author as well as a coach and teacher. I'm so grateful for the opportunity to walk through the doorway to share my gifts and my calling.

What do I mean by the title "The Doorways Of Life"?

Throughout our life, we have many transitions that we make. Birthdays, holidays, school graduations, employment, and so on. We have a choice of how to approach each phase or transition in our lives. In many ways, I see myself as a visual person. So, when it came time to think of topics to discuss and relate to, I thought about doors. We don't think much of them regarding our homes, places of work or business or shopping centers. However, when we start to relate them to areas in life, they take on a whole new meaning.

During our time of dating before being engaged, my wife asked me what my purpose was. Now this was a challenge for me. I had been coaching my whole life but didn't know that's what it was until I went to college. Friends, relatives, colleagues— many people gravitated to me because they knew I had their best interest at heart. I wanted to see them win.

In my conversations with people, I could easily turn it around and make them the subject. If someone asked me how I was doing, I saw that as a challenge. Give them a quick answer and then ask about them. Hit them with question after question, something I call "sincere deflection." Everyone fell for this. Except my wife. No one had ever asked me what my purpose was. I really had to think about this.

My answer? To help people find *their* purpose. Even my answer was a flip for me, an exercise in removing the spotlight from me and back onto the questioner. But I now understand why it took me so long to get to this place, where I am today. Could I have written this book earlier? Possibly. But what it has now is backing, experience, and a passion to help people express their gifts, recognize their surroundings, and take advantage of opportunities before them.

It took me a while to actually sit down to write this book. (I actually dictated some while walking, so in that case I was standing!) Initially, I lost some steam after completing half of it. My previous method of writing was compromised due to a software update, and I had to seek an alternative. Many people find that push in them when their back is up against a wall. Now, at the time of this writing, I'm not there, with my back against a wall. But I see what's next, and I see the doorway to live the life I want to live. A life where I help others stay focused. Where I help people dissolve procrastination and get results. And yes, I can speak on procrastination as much as anyone. In all my book buying, I've bought two books on procrastination and a handful of courses on focus. To date, the books remain not fully read, and the courses not yet started. Procrastination at its best!

But this book is a major accomplishment I want to share with the world. And you should know that by my next book, those courses will be completed, and those books will be read. The real question will be: did I employ the tools gained? What I've learned is that you can buy as many books and take as many courses as you want; however, it's putting to use the lessons learned that will show progress and bear fruit, move you to that next level. Buying a book on being a billionaire doesn't make you one. It's the tools you use consistently over time that get you to that goal line.

And that's my hope here. That this book becomes a tool for you to use on your journey of self-improvement and self-discovery. Although the first word of that term is "self," the impact that it has on those who put it to use is far-reaching.

My book coach/editor asked me what my purpose was in writing this book. I told her that my key purpose is to help people realize their potential and utilize their skills. And to hone those skills **and be able to** recognize when an opportunity comes for them to utilize them.

The reason I'm writing this book is to have people recognize the different phases in their lives and to offer them the best tools and equipment. I'm calling for them to step out of their comfort zone and to stretch beyond what they've done in the past, to rise to their next level. This is for anyone who has any type of goal regardless of what it may be.

I know many editors and book publishers look to see who your target audience is. I'm looking for those who are seeking ways to become unstuck and change their view, to gain new eyes and new hands to work with, a new way to walk. Those who want to operate on a different level of discernment and constantly improve themselves for the benefit of those around them.

Another term for target audience could be "tribe." It means a specific group of people who are aligned with your interests, want to learn from you, and desire your skill set. Now whether or not you make money from your association with the tribe or whether it's for research or for a nonprofit doesn't matter. These are the people you most align with and can connect you to other tribes with similar interests.

My quest for wisdom and self-improvement began early in life and it continues today when I can convey what I've learned and experienced to those who are hungry for wisdom. As a teacher and coach, the joy I receive is when I see the light go on and somebody gets how they can use what I've shared for their transformation. For accomplishing their goals. For being a light to those who are in still the dark. They choose to be modest enough to desire to be a change agent, but not cocky enough to know that their insight is the only light for some people.

My passion to help people grow is one of the reasons I wrote this book. It's also a result of my foray into social media with the intent to help people in a stuck place recognize the pathway to their next level of progress. What started as a video series ended up with what's in your hands—or on your e-reader! As someone who's keen on finding and using the best learning modality for people, I have future plans to have this content available in various formats including audio and video.

As someone who's into various forms and levels of communication, I understand that it's not just about speaking and writing. It's about the interpretation and re-phrasing of the suggestions and advice proffered here. Although please understand that language, structure, and quotes all come into play when I consider my writing style and how to convey the message of progress, solid transformation, and measured results.

This book is not just about putting words on paper. It's about transformative change that will ripple not only through those closest to you but will have a generational impact. For too long, many people have just dealt with what they see in front of them. However, I was undone when I discovered Dr.

Myles Munroe when he first said, "Sight is the enemy of vision."

That phrase stunned me, that sight is the enemy of vision. It opened my eyes to a new perspective. What you see can be a detriment to what you envision in your mind. If what you see is what you can imagine and it's limiting, then your vision gets smaller and doesn't go beyond what it was purposed to do.

Your mind doesn't have a filter. It only allows what you intentionally allow in. That what we see as common are anecdotes or symbols for life changes. Whether it's positive or negative, everything is seen as relative but can be used to the benefit of society as a whole.

An analogy would be the shark growing in a fish tank. It will only grow to the size of its environment. In the ocean, a shark will grow up to between 10 to 20 feet long. In an environment of a small lake or pond, a shark will only grow as big as the body of water and maybe become food for other fish that are more adept to that environment.

I ask you to read this book with an open mind. Be open to growth. Be open to change. Be open to the new. Be open to your transformation. Isn't it about time? And I'm looking forward to the results you obtain from reading and applying the principals put forth in this book. Know that they come from someone all too familiar with doorways and openings and how they can close when not acted upon in a timely manner. And how they open when you're open.

My heartfelt wish is for you to come away from this book with new eyes, a new perspective, and a plan on how to move to the next level in your journey. Here's to you opening the doorways of your life and your success!

Chapter One:
Your Doorway Out

Don't live FOR your dreams. Live FROM your dreams.

When it comes to achieving goals, the first step is to make progress. Movement and mere motion don't equal progress. It needs to be precise and towards a particular mark that moves you closer to your goals. However, before you take action, the first thing you should do is take inventory of your surroundings and what you have with as well. This includes people. You start to assess the utility of each item and make decisions on whether they're a help or a hindrance.

Realize that you need to find your way out of the situation you're in so you can move forward. But let's break this down.

The definition of a goal is to achieve something you haven't done before this. There's no blueprint. It's a mark in the distance. It looks nothing like where you currently are. Wherever you are in life now, you need to get out of it so you can move forward towards your goals. Thus, the title of this chapter "Your Doorway Out."

Many times, it takes a certain amount of emphasis for us to change our perspective. The above quote, for example, highlights what I like to call the "Power of the Preposition." "For" and "From" have two distinctive meanings, thus the capitalization. If you live FOR something, then you're in a constant chase towards it. Your actions, your speech, your way of life dictates your move towards that dream. As time passes, it either gets closer or it remains just out of reach. The passage of time can also bring frustration and depression as it may cause you to compare yourself to others who are already living their dream.

If you live FROM your dream, it becomes your source. You're now living a different life and making moves in alternate ways. Why? Because you're pulling in whatever fits your dream vs. chasing after it. Perspective now dictates your speech, education, tribe, and progress. You have your dream; now you're bringing it into the physical.

You can open the door to a certain room. Or you can close the door to a certain issue in your life. Doors can play a key element in our lives whatever goals we're wanting to achieve. If we want to be healthy, we might need to close the door to bad food such as snacks, chips, or ice cream while we open the door to healthier choices like vegetables, plant-based diets, and preservative-free foods.

If you want to learn an instrument, you need to close the door to distractions and open the door to practicing, as well as diligence and consistency. You might choose to pay for a teacher to help you to learn that instrument or go online and watch videos. Open the door to committing time to access your goal.

Or it could be you want to start a business. So, you need to close the door to those people who put doubts in your mind about what you can accomplish. And open a door to those who can help you achieve your goal.

The first doorway we all encounter is shortly after we're born. We may not be cognizant of it, but it's there. Some may even say that our birth is the first doorway that we come across. It's literally our entrance into the world.

You're first formed inside the womb. There begins your development: limbs, lungs, blood vessels, brain, and all organs. You gain nutrition through the umbilical cord. Also, you begin to recognize sounds, voices, and all stimuli in your environment. Now, you're not cognizant of this nor can you bring up those memories. But it is happening. As you grow, your current abode becomes smaller to the point that you must now seek

19

alternate living arrangements. Your current landlord is kicking you out and with good reason. You've outgrown your current living space.

Not only are you being kicked out but you're also being pushed out. Seems that your residence has a mind of its own and wants to push you along the way. Now, you have the choice to cooperate or be yanked out of your home. Either way, you're getting out.

As you travel down this tunnel, there doesn't appear to be an opening, an exit, someplace for you to go. Unsure of yourself, you go headfirst as you burst through into another world. Yes, it's cold out there and very unfamiliar. But soon, you hear a voice that you've heard your whole life. It's familiar and soothing. You scream until you get close to it. As soon as you're there, you also feel a familiar rhythm. One that has been with you since you became aware. Now, all is right with the world. Thank goodness that you went through that doorway.

By the way, no need to sue the landlord or bring her up on any charges. Just call her "Mom." In light of this, we need to understand how doors help us transition in life and in business.

If you investigate the fields of therapy and psychology, you'll find that most people seek help to discover areas of themselves that may be wounded or challenged and receive healing. Those areas have been referenced in those fields as rooms. Even when you're transitioning to another space, the term often used is "closing the door."

So, it's important to gain understanding about the impact doorways have in our lives. As you continue to read, examine how each topic applies to you. Until we're no longer breathing, it's our responsibility to ourselves and others to define our current state and know when to look for the doorway.

As I close out this chapter, I want to make sure that there's an understanding on how your journey will happen and how it will move forward. Using doorways as a metaphor, the point is to expand your vision and horizon as you set goals. Change your perspective. Once you stretch, you can never go back to where you were before. Once the brain is stretched, it can't return to its previous form.

As you progress, it's important for you to take the Cortés method. You may recall this method was where Hernán Cortés had a few men and they needed to conquer an island. There were thousands of natives there. Cortés knew he had to incentivize his men to fight like their lives depended upon it. So, in the middle of the night, he burned the boats going home. When the men woke up and realized what he had done, they knew their only option was to move forward and fight to survive and thrive in this new land. Of course, they won because they had nothing to go back to.

And that's what you need to do. Once you go through a particular door it may be essential for you to light a match to it so it's no longer an option to go back but to move forward.

My desire is that as you read this book, you'll see the full application of the analogy of the doors and doorways and how they apply to your life.

QUESTIONS TO CONSIDER
Where are you currently and where would you like to be?
Have you identified the doorway out and into your next position in life?

Chapter Two:
Gaining Access

Access is a privilege that is given or granted,
never taken.

Years ago, I was hired as a manager. I was looking forward to my own team and how I could mold them. I first had to go through Human Resources (HR). Now, if you've never had a job or it has been a while since you've went through the orientation and onboarding process of working for a new company, let me clue you in. HR is your first stop and sets the tone to your first day. You have to bring ID, dress your best, and remember to enter into the building with a state of confusion. Signage can be poor, and you need to ask several people for directions to the front door. Once you find it, you enter the lobby area and are greeted by security who ask you to sign in. But before you can just walk in, they have someone come down and get you to let you in. Though it's your first day, you don't have access to the building yet.

Once you sign the documents and agree to their terms, then you gain access—access to the building, to their computer system, and their proprietary work.

Unless there's a document on file that's in line with the structure of their organization, only then will you have access.

When it comes to gaining access, much of that is based on who you know, what you know, and how you use that information. Now some access should be denied due to the volatility of the materials in the hands of an inexperienced person. An example would be a laboratory. If someone is inexperienced, they could mix the wrong chemicals together and cause injury or even a lethal event.

It's the same when it comes to your thoughts, beliefs, and emotions. But the challenge is that there may not be any type of warning when it comes to those materials. You'll find there's a point in time when you must determine what it means to gain access. There are certain rules or stipulations you should follow and measure up to in order for you to be given such a privilege. Those are obstacles that are meant to hold you back as well as open your eyes to what's more of a detriment than a help. When you want to gain something that means you've been without. So, you're looking to making an addition to what you currently possess. What got you here isn't enough to get you to that next level. It's key that you gain all the equipment and tools needed for you to be prepared to learn, grow, and develop. And to open your eyes to insight and understandings that will stretch you to a point from which you can't return.

Let's talk more about access being a privilege. A privilege is defined as "a special rights advantage, something only granted to a particular person or group." Know that privilege is something that's earned. It means you're in a special class and you've achieved a particular level of education, calling, or insight. Depending on what your goal is, the access you seek to gain involves attracting a particular target. If you want to live a healthier lifestyle, then you need to reach a certain level of exercise and eating that will help you gain access to insights that turn your achievements from temporary to permanent. In order for it to be a true gain, there's a need for you to measure exactly where you are to determine what access you need.

In the corporate world, certain titles and promotions determine the level of access. A manager has a different level of access than a director or a supervisor. Usually, the leadership ranking is supervisor to manager to director, then from director to senior director to vice president. Each comes with its own level of access and responsibilities. Once you gain access, there's a level of responsibility that comes with that so you're protective of the information you now have at your fingertips.

What first comes to mind about access and privilege is what you bring to the table. So, for you to gain access, you should have an understanding of the gifts and skillset you bring that can be an addition and an asset instead of a liability. You also want to make sure that when you're vying for the opportunity to gain access, you've done your due diligence and made sure this is the right door for you to gain access to. There are some doors you go into that will give you access but aren't the right choices for you. A mistake can cost you time, money, and lost opportunities that may have been available had you not gone into this particular room. You need to do your best to ascertain the room or level you're requesting access to. Does it fit within your needs? Does it line up with the dream you're living from? Are you in alignment with the thoughts and actions generated from your dreams?

For instance, you may need money, so you rob a bank or a series of stores. Now that money could be to finance your dream. However, when you're caught and sentenced to serve time, you lose time and money as well as opportunity, because you now must pay your debt to society and the penal system. While you can still use that time to review and plan your actions upon release, it's still a massive detour that could have been avoided had you reviewed alternative options that were legal and obtainable by proper means.

Sometimes a gain must come at a loss. That means there may be something you need to lose or get rid of to gain the accessibility to achieve your dreams. For instance, to gain focus, you have to lose the spirit of procrastination. To learn how to run a four-minute mile, you need to lose your desire to watch TV and stay up until midnight. As you're learning and refining yourself to achieve that goal, you realize that one of the key parts of developing the four-minute mile is the proper amount of sleep. So, this shows you that a gain can necessitate a loss so it can make room for the proper access needed for achievement.

Now you understand that access can be granted, not based on who you are, but who you have become, or who you are becoming. There's a recognition of progress and forward motion that now opens the door to your next level. Access is precious and it's something that needs to be considered and handled carefully. It's about understanding the level of clearance you have. There are many TV shows about certain government operatives who need to be eliminated because they had a level of clearance they no longer need. So, the question becomes: What will you do when you have the success? How will you handle it? Are you able to use it for good and to increase the success of those around you? Or will you be a detriment and become the enemy of those you're initially trying to help? Before you fight for what you feel is your right, begin to ascertain your need to gain access to this particular area. Only then will you be able to determine and make the right decision you need for proper and precise achievement.

ACCESS DENIED

If it doesn't open, then it's not your door. To gain access, it's important to note that what you used to get you here may not get you there. It's going to take new tactics and new actions for you to gain access. This means you need to talk to a community that has a similar mindset as you, but on a higher plane. Those around you can dictate your level of access and vertical movement. In other words, get with people who are already where you want to be. Once you've connected with this group, note that there's a certain level of communication that comes with it. It's not about what you say, but how it's received. So, as you speak, you need to not only note what you're saying, but note the main modality of reception that the tribe adheres to. Don't aim to win them over with your personality or monetary compensation. Work your way in with sincere intentions and by adding value to the community. Whatever your dream is, whatever your goal is, whatever your intentions are, let them know. Be sure that the position you're in aligns with their best interest. The goal is to improve the livelihood of your tribe. If your goal is to be healthier, to learn a language, to buy a house, or to live on a budget, then you can frame your request for access by noting that this will make you a better human being and be of better use for those who can benefit from your expertise.

Understand that gaining access is not for you to dominate and subjugate but to improve and help others become invaluable tools to their local, regional, and global society.

TO ADD VALUE TO OTHERS, BELIEVE IN YOUR VALUE

When working within the community looking to see what you can add, one key is to believe in your value. You must believe you have something that's needed, that you can offer which will prove to be a positive addition to the community you're attempting to gain access to. When looking at the talents and gifts you bring to the table, you have to adjust your belief system to believe they have value in your specific arena. You don't know all 7.2 billion people on Earth. So, you can't assume that what you have to offer won't be of value. The only way it becomes worthless is in what you attribute to it. If someone has said you don't have value, you need to identify the source and remove it from having any room in your mind. The only power that particular source has is what you give it. If you immediately remove any power and authority that was given to it in the past, it will cease to exist. Your value assignment is not based on the thoughts or opinions of others but on what you believe for yourself. So, when you're looking at what you can give in order to gain access, I encourage you to put yourself on a higher plane. People tend to underestimate their gifts and the impact they can have on others.

Now I'm not encouraging you to be dogmatic or high minded to the point of being obnoxious when sharing your values. Far from it. You need to operate with a mindset of humility and grace. You know your worth. You know you have something to contribute that no one else can. Everyone has their own experiences in life. When you meet someone, it's not just them you're meeting. You're meeting everything they've gone through, every situation they've had to overcome, every challenge they've surpassed, every issue currently challenging them. You can bring up your thoughts even if they're not complete.

However, there might be something within them that contributes to others as each person has a distinct key to unlock different doors that give you the right access.

Stay true to yourself and what you have to offer. When you operate with assurance and sincerity, those elements will guide you and seep into your words regardless of order or mis-speech. Those around you will be able to relate to your spirit and your feelings that exude from your words and actions. Words have an impact but so do the corresponding actions. The relief comes when you finally hear the words you've worked so hard for: access granted. Come into your next level and take action.

ACCESS AS A RIGHT

I spoke earlier about access being the ability to enter into a place. But access is also defined as permission, the ability or the right to approach to answer or speak with a person. So, there's somebody who may have the answer to your next level in life. The question becomes: Do you have access to that person? Or do you have access to that group? Notice that it's fine to get approval if permission is granted for that to happen. You don't just approach in any old way. For instance, when dealing with royalty or high levels of government officials, there's a certain protocol you need to follow to speak to the king or official. Any movements or procedures you take that go against those principles in place could cause you to insult or show disrespect. Such an act against the throne or executive office brings the danger of being jailed, fined, or finding your life in jeopardy. When you approach a king, it's customary to bring a gift to show deference to the throne. Your goal is to gain access to the King and all that belongs to him and what comes with him. To do so, you have to consult with someone, so you know the proper steps to take and what to wear so as not to be an affront.

In the Bible is a story about Queen Esther who went through a one-year period of prepping herself in order to be ready to come before the King. She studied with her uncle who schooled her on the best way to be when going before royalty. The previous Queen went against the protocol and didn't approach the King when he called on her. The King was immediately enraged and called forth someone to replace her. That's where Esther entered the scene. She went through six months of physical and mental prep to have a brief audience with the King. But the preparation she went through and the training she got from her uncle would have an impact on her people and would go beyond what she could imagine. Not only was her physical appearance an attribute but also the spirit with which she came in, one of humility and respect, with deference and mindfulness of the magnitude of the King. When the King recognized that the gratitude and respect was upon her and the spirit she carried, she was given an open audience before him. Anything less and she may not have been received. So, your prep is important, how you approach a matter or a person and what spirit with which you come in to gain access to your doorway to the next level.

QUESTIONS TO CONSIDER

Is access to your life something you give discreetly or without care?

Has there been anyone who has used or abused their access to you?

Chapter Three:
Importance of Keys

Small keys can unlock big doors.

For years, I've dealt with the constant fear of losing my keys. I'm not sure what that's about. Yet, I can tell you where I think it comes from. So many times, I've heard of people losing their keys. Either they went out partying the night before, or they were in a rush in the morning and not sure where they put them.

What sticks out in my mind is the sense of panic and urgency that comes with that. The person doesn't know what to do. They've lost access. They have no authority. Their whole day has been turned upside down because they can't find their keys. What also accompanies that urgency is the fact that it's not just one key. They've lost the key ring, which includes their keys to their house, car, back door, parent's house, office, etc. It's the immediate loss of access that scares them. I've heard so many stories of people being stuck outside their home or who have locked themselves outside of their cars. Now they have to call a friend, relative, or security service to help them get out of their jam. Until that time comes, they're out of sorts. I don't ever want to be put in that predicament.

When it comes to keys, I'm very careful. I put them in the same pants pocket. They have a designated place I put them when I return home. I even make sure that if I have keys in my hand and I'm walking outside, I grip them extra tightly. Especially when I walk over or near a sewer or grate. The fear is that deep.

You know the importance keys have in our physical life. Now let's discuss the impact of keys in our metaphorical lives. What is the purpose of keys? Keys give you access. Access as I previously defined it is entry, permission, an allowance to an area. When we think of access, we understand there are different levels of access. Certain office buildings require you to have a keycard to enter the building. That same keycard may be needed to access your floor, depending on the work you do and/or the security of the building.

Certain executives may have access to private bathrooms, gyms, or showers. So, it depends upon the level of access you have. Bottom line: keys are essential to gaining access. Keys help you to unlock doors. And keys help you to lock doors. I discussed the importance of access in the previous chapter.

But it's important to have the right key. Shape doesn't matter. You want to hear the lock unclick or see the green light. If there's a goal you want to obtain, you need to figure out how to open that door, the place you haven't been. What are the keys or key you need to get there?

For example, if you want to accomplish a particular goal, you need to ask, "Okay, what is the key? Where do I find the key? How do I obtain it?" It might be that you have to take a class, one that will equip you with the right tools to find the key to gain access to your next level. You may have to study under someone to gain their expertise. This could entail a mentor-mentee relationship where you seek out an expert who has gained success in where you want to go.

You may need to read a particular book, study its contents, and incorporate the information into your life to find the key. Depending on your style of learning, it might even include an audiobook, that you listen to in the car, or during your walk, jog, or bike ride. The key may also come in the form of a video or video series. It's important to know your best format of learning and follow it so you can gain understanding and proper application of the contents.

The goal is that you want to find access to the next phase of your life, so you're searching to find the way. To get into this particular phase or room that will help you achieve your goal, it's important that you have the right key. So, understand that keys give you access. Keys give you power. Keys give you authority.

What's also important is to find out if you have the correct doorway to open. Sometimes keys can open multiple doors. But do you need to go into every room? If you're in a hallway with several doors and one key fits them all, you'll spend time opening each to see if it's the right room for you. That could be wasted time that you could be using to improve yourself. You need to become an expert at not only finding the right key but determining what door you need to open.

Once you determine this is the door you want to open, that this is a doorway you're going to walk through, you're now back to your keys. Which key do you need to open that door? At times, you may say, "My key may be that I want to live a different life." It could be that you want to change your belief system, so which key do you need for that? Do you need to read a book? Do you need an accountability coach? Do you need a therapist or a counselor? Do you need just one person?

Do you need to join a group if that's where you want to be? It's important to discover the dynamic(s) you need to grow and develop. Some people thrive in a single person setting, while others prefer a group meeting, whether small, medium, or large. Do you prefer in person, virtual, or hybrid? Once that determination is made, you can see that the keys have the power and authority to help you transition to your next life commitment, phase, or level. That's just a sample of what happens when you find the right key.

LONG TERM KEY

Years ago, I had a job where I trained executives, VPs, and staff on budget software. I did this for over six years. To say I liked this job was an understatement. It felt like a hidden need I didn't know I had.

Prior to this job the cable company rang my doorbell one day and said they were there to install our system. After they spent some time doing that, the technician came to me and walked me through the system. He said our plan now included something called a DVR. He explained that this was a way for us to record not only the show we were watching but future shows as well. So, I was watching TV and applying for jobs. A show came on called "Man versus Food." For those not familiar with the show, the host would visit three restaurants. The last restaurant would have a food contest and he would see if he could win. I became intrigued with the show. What I liked about it was the restaurants in the featured dishes.

While I was watching this, I decided to pull up a Word document and make note of the name of the restaurant and the featured dish as well as the location. I also started discovering other shows about food options and paradises like Pizza Paradise, Breakfast Paradise, and Hamburger Paradise. My list got longer. My DVR started filling up with food shows from the Food Network and the travel network. Presently, my list is over 60 pages with a number of restaurants and featured dishes. Lo and behold with my new job, I was in a position where I needed to travel and train others on software. The cool thing about that was that I would be in a location for four or five days. Yes, I had a per diem and I also had a list of famous spots to dine in.

As I traveled, I saw a lot of interaction between guests and security. This included airports, rental agencies, hotels, or restaurants. What I learned best was that I would have a better interaction with individuals if I smiled and asked about their day. People care less about what you need until they know you care. If I could make them smile, then my travel experience would be that much smoother. Having that knowledge served as an important key to my success in that position.

So, this is key when you're transitioning into another phase and going through a doorway. What you say—whether you're typing or speaking to someone directly or indirectly—is important to your experience in that room, at that level, in that phase.

"Doors of the future are open to those who know how to push them."- Coluche

When I was doing my research for this book, I found this quote. It got me thinking about various types of doors and how they open. Most times we're accustomed to manual doors that have a handle on them. Now even the handle isn't an indicator as to whether we need to pull or push. We only find that out with trial and error. But there are different types of doors that are manual that open without a handle. I've seen this type of door for a restroom. This would be a door you push to go through. Some type of marking or a plate is on the door to indicate this is where your hand goes to push it open.

However, I also thought about pet doors. For those who have dogs or cats that go in and out as they see fit, you know that door doesn't open vertically but horizontally. Either way, you open it by pushing at the bottom versus the side of the door. So, pets must be taught how to enter and exit. It's also the job of the committed owner to handle the training of their pet.

When I was younger, we had to go through fire training at my school. We had fire drills and we needed to know what to do in case there was an emergency. I remember the school running two to three drills a year to make sure this was in compliance with state ordinance.

One of the key rules they taught us was to test the doorknob to see what the temperature was. If it was cold, it was okay to go through. But if it was hot, then we needed to stay where we were and put a towel underneath the doorknob. They emphasized that the temperature check was essential to our ability to survive the fire.

It was important that we all knew this because no one was selected as the lead in an emergency. The expectation was that we were all aware and knew what to do. It's the same when you're progressing through a doorway on your way to your forward movement. You want to check the door to see how to open it. Is there a class you need to take? Is there a particular word or phrase you need to speak? Is there someone who's been through that door before and can give you insight on the best way and time to open it? These are critical factors and questions you want to ask in order for you to achieve success.

Earlier I spoke about lost keys. Now many people know the feeling they get when they lose their keys. They feel dread, fear, or defeat. You look around your house and in your bags and drawers. The longer it takes, the more irrational you get. You begin to tear the house apart to find those keys. You play the blame game, and everyone becomes a suspect regardless of age. Doesn't matter if they were even in the house at the time the keys came up missing. Your soul is not at rest and your spirit is disturbed. Everyone around you can feel the tension coming off you as you frantically search for this set of keys that accesses either your car or home.

That's how palpable it gets. You've seen it before. Someone can walk into your house as you're looking around and they know the environment is off immediately. So, they ask you what's wrong. Your response, your face, and your body are in unison in this tense level of searching. Your environment shifts, everything stops until you locate these keys. You've now experienced this loss of power, this loss of access. Nothing will abate it until these keys are found. That's how important keys are to your life.

QUESTIONS TO CONSIDER

Are there keys in your life that you have been using incorrectly?

Have you shared those keys with everyone in your life or just a select few?

Chapter Four:
Types of Doorways

Once you know the type,
then you'll know what's right.

Now, this analogy has some dependence on where you live. But let's move beyond that. When we start learning to walk, we focus on gaining the correct footing. What helps us is the lesson of falling. Yes, such a wonderful teacher, falling. Even as a child, we realize that falling is something we have to do. No experimentation, secret laboratories, focus groups, or placebos needed.

Falling has that jarring impact that immediately creates an impression in our brains. We tell ourselves, "No, I don't want to do this again. What must I do to keep this from happening?" Then we focus on how to walk without falling.

We grow accustomed to going from room to room. We cross thresholds at whim until we encounter a door. In most homes, we must apply pressure (push or pull) to get that door open. So, we're familiar with manual doors.

Ever see a child when it's their first time out of the house? Let's say their mom has them by the hand and they're walking. They have a picture of their home in their head and are applying it to the outside world. Thus, the term "looking at the world through a child's eyes."

We know in general that we have to apply pressure to open the door. As we approach a big building while out walking which is massive in our young eyes, something happens. The doors just open. What happened? Where are the knobs, the hinges? This is an introduction to automatic doors for our ever-learning mind.

Let's take this analogy and apply it to our lives and goals. What type of door do you have in front of you? Do you have an automatic door? Do you have a manual door? What's the difference?

AUTOMATIC DOORS

An automatic door means you need to position yourself in front of it so it can sense you and open. Let's get into the mind of the designer for a minute. One guess at the purpose of automatic doors was to make the entry more accessible to those seeking access. Whether your hands were full or not wasn't a concern. Instead of exerting energy to pull and grasp a door handle or knob, the designer would rather that energy go elsewhere. If it's a store, it would be buying more products. In an office building, it's keeping you focused on the business.

To get the doors to open automatically, you need to be in a particular position. Anything outside that designated area won't trigger entry. This applies to your life when you're transitioning, when you're creating, and when you're going to the next level. It could be regarding attaining a goal, starting a business, living a healthier lifestyle, writing a book, or getting higher learning and a certificate.

When you're transitioning, you need to look at the circumstances. Observe what's coming in and position yourself to receive it. Position yourself so when the door opens for you, you're able to walk right in. Positioning is important, especially when it's an automatic door. If you're out of alignment or unaware of the area where you should be, those doors remain closed. You can become frustrated, angry, or develop serious angst if you think you're taking the right action.

You may start thinking that the door is at fault when it's you who hasn't learned the mechanics of the door. The door is neither right nor wrong. Neither is your goal. They're not imbued with these qualities. It's you, the one seeking entrance who must make sure you're correctly positioned for access and entry.

So, position yourself to understand what's showing up around you. Understand your environment so you can receive access and can walk through.

MANUAL DOORS

Now, the second type is a manual door, and they're not relegated to only homes anymore. Stores and office buildings are included as well. With a manual door, you either push or pull. No sensors are in a manual door like they are in the automatic door. So, there's no particular position you need to be in to open the door. Although there is an ideal one. The first *Lord of The Rings* movie comes to mind. The Hobbits had doors where the knob was in the middle. Peculiar, but part of their culture.

The manual door can have a knob, a handle, or neither. You need to know what the action is for you to go through to your next level. You have to perform a physical action in order to push that door open so you can transition.

Before even considering the action, be sure you have the proper mindset. That entails clearing your mind from past obstacles and making sure you're open to any path that presents itself.

Often times, we limit our view by our past experiences. To gain the correct perspective, there's a level of intentionality you need to operate from when deciding on the next action for increase. Once you've come to that understanding, many actions will cause the manual door to open.

It could be that you have to take a course that will give you the knowledge needed to push through. You may have to sign up with a coach who will help you in opening the door so you can transition. The coach would assist you to highlight your strengths and improve challenging areas regarding your approach.

Maybe it's a video or a series of videos that open you up to new avenues for transitioning to your next level of progress. You may choose to read a particular book that helps you gain understanding on the manual door in front of you. However, here's where you can get stuck in a certain mindset. Often, when people hear about a type of goal or making progress, and it involves a book, and it's often a self-improvement book. Yet, your breakthrough may come from a novel, a textbook, a biography, or even poetry. You need to be completely open to various pathways that inspiration and guidance can come to you.

You may have to do a specific exercise if your goal is to get in better shape. This exercise or series of exercises may not even be in your sphere of knowledge. So, to search for the right exercise, you need to set the tone in your mind. That tone must be enjoyment and removal of the fear of abandoning familiar surroundings to go beyond your visual landscape.

You may have to commit some time to practice a language or an instrument. Deliberateness and intention go hand in hand when this becomes your goal. But it's important to open that door so you can walk through it and ascend to your next level. You have to determine what the action is that will get to that next level. Do you need to reach out and open that door or do you need to position yourself? Consider this when you're transitioning.

Your goals and vision are causing you and calling you to operate on a higher level of understanding. I've said it before, and I'll say it again. What got you here isn't enough to get you to where you want to go. You need to begin to dress in the present in the clothes of the future. You need to begin to talk and speak as if your future has already been accomplished. When you speak that way, your mind now comes to a new level of thinking. You begin to see those closed doors as an annoyance. Your toleration level lowers dramatically. Where you're going doesn't have the means or the fashion for incomplete sentences, actions, or people. This may sound harsh, but this is where you have to go to get what you want. Your desires would suffer if the doors remained open and allowed the nonsense and garbage of the past that holds you back, to get in.

Let's talk about positioning in a different scenario. Imagine you're a special team's number on a football team. Many positions need the right individual for that role. One position is called the returner. This person does kickoff returns and punt returns. They're so specialized in what they do, that they're on a particular unit on the team called Special Teams.

If you've ever watched a football game, you would see this person called out after a scoring situation or a failed attempt for the opposing team to get a first down. This person has an important job which depends on positioning. Let's examine this. Their first position is to properly catch the ball after it's been kicked to them or an area near them. This role is multifaceted in its responsibilities. The returner must be aware of his surroundings including the people coming towards him, where he stands on the field, and his ability to advance the ball from the point of the catch. He has to make quick decisions in a short amount of time so he can get himself and his team in the proper position.

Depending upon where the ball was kicked, he needs to decide if he's going to try to advance his position or keep what's given to him. His goal is to put his team in the best area possible so they can advance and score. If he decides to run the ball, he has to now follow his projected path with the hopes that his fellow teammates will be able to block the opposing team from tackling him. His objective is to score. His secondary objective is to get his team in a scoring position.

As you can see, positioning is the primary responsibility for this role. Without an understanding of that, the player will always be at a loss and be a danger to his team's chances of winning. Most likely, he will be cut because of his lack of understanding.

This is how it is when it comes to manual doors. I use this as a metaphor to potential opportunities to achieve your goal. When the chance comes for you to be in an area of reception, will you be in the proper position and know what to do upon receipt?

The positions of the punt returner and kickoff returner are very important. It's not just catching the ball, but it's how the other limbs are positioned. For example, how are the feet placed? Are they crossed? Are they close together? Are they shoulder-width apart? Each of those positions produce a different result when the ball comes. Once the runner catches, he has to be in a position to advance. The first two positions are a no. The runner can't advance when his legs are crossed or close together because he lacks stability and the capacity to push off in case of an advancing tackler. He's compromised from the start and has placed himself in a position of playing defense versus offense.

I'm a movie buff, a big fan of movies that have the underdog winning. Many times, I see scenes where the wealthy people are checking into a hotel. They get out of a fancy car or limo. They have someone holding the door for them as they enter the hotel, and a bell boy is bringing up the luggage. Someone makes sure their room is immaculate. Even as they go to their room, they have someone opening the door for them. Now I look at this as the concierge service.

We've talked about manual doors and automatic doors but what this hotel image came to me was about a doorman. What's hindering your progress in life? Is it about a person or persons who can help you as you transition to your next level? Could this person be a mentor? A mentor could be a colleague or a manager or a boss in your place of employment. Your mentor's goal is to help in equipping you so you're ready for this next level.

Also, they are there to be your doorman. Now regardless of the title, the doorman plays an essential part in your progress towards your goal. They are the ones who will hold the door open for you as you go through it with any tools you need to continue to grow into your next season. That doorman is someone who has not only equipped you but is also seen as part of your team. We all need someone to help us in reaching our goals as we move along through life. This person is a critical component to teach us and expand our perspective when it comes to our next doorway.

As I mentioned earlier, the very first doorway we encounter is the birth canal. No one is born alone. There's a team of doctors, nurses, and medical professionals there to assist you as you enter the world. Even if you had a home birth, you still had someone there to bring you into the physical world. Your transition from the womb to the world was successful and equipped you to live and be productive. That person not only helped you, but they also helped prepare your parents throughout this journey while you were growing in the womb. Though that doorway you were being assisted into the world by a team that had your best interests at heart.

IF OPPORTUNITY DOESN'T KNOCK, BUILD A DOOR

Back in 1903, an industrial change necessitated the need for the horse-and-buggy to be retired. Henry

Ford saw an opportunity to mass produce a mechanical device known as an automobile that would no longer need or require the use of a horse and carriage. When his cars came online, his main purpose was for them to be used by the ultra-wealthy and by companies that needed to transport goods in a faster manner. So, unless you fit into either of those categories you were just a spectator and not a participant. Mr. Chrysler saw this as an opportunity to advance and make cars not only for the ultra-wealthy but for the everyday family member. Now initially there was no interest from the family members as they saw this as an unneeded expense. However, Mr. Chrysler felt the necessity to build the door even though opportunity had not yet knocked.

So, he took his time to build and create an affordable automobile that could be priced and used by anyone who had a business idea and could use this for the transportation. As soon as his vehicles were available, they became the hottest commodity to own in the US. Not only were they the in-thing to have but also, they sparked a revolution throughout the rest of the world. Japan became a huge maker and exporter of vehicles.

Today many opportunities and options exist when it comes to vehicle purchase. Levels of vehicles are available for the ultra-wealthy as well as for those who operate on a particular budget and demographic. The point of this is that there is an opportunity out there for you. There's another level for you to rise to. In your search for a door, it may be necessary for you to build one. When you don't find what you need, you build with what you have. Yes, this will go outside of your norm, but it's necessary for you to raise yourself and your mindset to the next level. You just need to get the skills required to make sure that door is going to where you need it to go and is constructed properly for you to walk through it.

QUESTIONS TO CONSIDER

Do you know the type of door you're dealing with, or do you need to build one?
Have you made sure you're in the right position to go through your next doorway?

Chapter Five:
The Purpose of Hallways

Whether it's noticed or not, there's a purpose to everything and for everything.

There's a TV show that includes as part of the opening montage, a group of lawyers walking down a hallway discussing what might be a case. Ever been a student in a class and got called out to the hallway? Or a teacher was asked to step out into the hall for a "quick" discussion? In both instances, it was the same place but was used for different reasons. The first one has the potential to receive some form of punitive judgment. In the second example, the hallway serves as a place to relay some vital news to the teacher that may or may not have an impact on the class. These are just some examples of the usage of a hallway. Let's get into our discussion for this chapter.

Years ago, I was ordained as a Deacon of a particular church. That church went through a transition, and I ended up changing to a new church home. I was asked to be a member of that Deacon Board as well. During my tenure as a board member, I sat in and participated in many meetings. Not only was I a board member, but I also served on other boards and ministries as well. One of the key positions I was elected to was that of Chairman of the Board. In all my meetings, whether they turned out good or bad, a key element was the conversation in the hallway. There was a lot of talking in meetings, but most of the critical conversations happened prior to them. Whether it was scheduled or not, many issues were accomplished in those hallway conversations. I say this to emphasize the importance of the hallway in that transition period between rooms.

When you're opening a door, sometimes you walk into your room. The room may be the next phase, the next level you need to reach your goal. Or it could be the final goal. But at times that door may lead to a hallway. A hallway is an area used to transition from one room to another. It's also defined as a corridor, a waiting area before going into a room. The hallway is the transition before you get into that next phase.

When you hear about a hallway, you may not pay any attention to it. It just seems like a passageway from one room to another, without any significance. But as noted in our examples, the hallway holds great significance and can be used to determine next steps. It can also be used as an area to weigh your options after having receiving advice or counsel.

In a doctor's office, for example, the hallway may be used as a waiting area before being seen. Depending on the purpose of the appointment, you can use the hallway in several ways.

1. Calming your nerves. The purpose of your appointment may be to discuss the result of a test from your previous visit.
2. Making a decision. You may have to make one after having been given your options for treatment for a particular ailment.
3. Being patient. You may need a place to either develop patience or for your impatience to grow. That may also include frustration as well.

Sometimes you're asked to come in early for your appointment. If you have a 1:30 pm appointment, you may be asked to come at 1:15 pm to fill out paperwork or do blood work. But if it's now 2:00 pm and you haven't been seen for any of the above, the circumstances are trying your patience. Now, you're weighing your options: leave and re-schedule or walk up to the front desk and complain. Or maybe another alternative. Either way, you're beginning to see the significance the hallway holds in various circumstances.

Now, let's focus on your transformative process. When it comes to hallways, they're treated more as an opportunity to steel yourself between phases of progression and transitions. For instance, if you're starting a business and you took a course to help you set up your business, you may get the certificate for the course. What's your next period? One of transition, the hallway. In this hallway, you have a new element added to your skillset that will play a pivotal part in your progress. You can now decide how to implement this certificate, so it maximizes your chances of proper preparation for the next room. Then you need to figure out your next steps.

HALLWAYS AS A RESET

Hallways give you the time to take inventory, to take stock of your position. You can also reset in a hallway and then see how you can prepare for that next phase. You get an opportunity to pull yourself together. The example that bests suits this is going from a parked car and running in a rainstorm with your umbrella up to the office building. Just as you step inside, you look around and realize that you're in the hallway entrance and have five minutes before your interview and/or presentation.

There, in that hallway, you close your umbrella and shake yourself off. You take some time to gather yourself. This gathering moment is crucial as you need to transition from running through a storm to a presentation/interview mindset.

So, as you're in that hallway taking stock, looking yourself over. This is where you don't want to rush. Take inventory. Review your goals. Review the steps you need. Here are some questions you can ask yourself.

- What do I need?
- Who can help me?
- What can assist me?
- What book or video do I need to prepare for that next step?
- What do I need to do around me and my environment?
- Is there something I need to put up on my wall or mirror to see every day?
- Is there a reminder I need to put on my phone?

It's crucial to note that there's a specific time to gather yourself. But don't take too long. The hallway isn't a resting area or a destination for long periods of time. It's a holding place, a location that has you using it effectively to pull yourself together. Don't be discouraged by hallways. If you open the door and you enter hallway, that's a transition.

Time can also be seen as a hallway. You would be surprised at the subliminal and literal programming that surrounds and spans beyond generations. It's the sayings we hear on a continuous basis that become ingrained in our thoughts and actions. Oftentimes, they create goals in our lives that run counterintuitive to our dreams and inspiration.

Whether it's television, the Internet, or social media, there are influences all around us. We need to become more mindful of what and who becomes our model and source of direction. If we're not careful, we can get lost and lose years of our lives driving towards a particular purpose that's not our own.

REAL-LIFE HALLWAY EXAMPLE

When I was younger, I was told the importance of going to school. I had to make sure my homework was done. I had to make sure I participated in class and that I took excellent notes. As I progressed in primary school, the next focus was high school. After that came the push to go to college. Back in those days, the push by our parents was to take the SATs and get a good score so we could get into college. We had to spend hours upon hours studying for these tests. We had to take classes that the school deemed necessary for us to be successful to gain entrance into the collegiate lifestyle.

The expectation was that when you graduated high school, you would immediately attend college. There was no pause or waiting period between the time you graduated and the beginning of the freshman semester, except for summer. But by the time graduation came around, you were expected to have an acceptance letter and have made a decision on what college you were attending in the fall. These were expectations put on us by our family, friends, teachers, and society.

This programming existed for many years. And in my opinion, it has done a disservice to hundreds of thousands of students. The reason is because the focus of entry into the collegiate life is the SATs. This standardized test focuses on two areas: math and English.

The challenge is: what if you're not smart in either? What if you're gifted in dance? What if you're mechanically inclined? What if you have a desire to be a landscaper? Where are the areas on the SATs that measure those skillsets?

I think one of the greatest innovations is the idea of the transition school, otherwise known as the Gap year. If you check statistics, you may see that there's a rise in students who decide to take off a year before going into college. Why is that?

We hear about huge college debt and the tough decision about choosing a major. The pressure is on. You've been in school for 12 years. You should probably know by now what you're going to pick for your major. You could have a career and a focus, because of what you've been through. There shouldn't be any pause about your going to college. Your major should already be laid out. Since the expectation is there, you decide to go based on what seems right and proper to those around you. You've taken the SAT. You see your friends and know what they want to do. So, you go along to get along. You move forward and say you're going to college because this is what you should do. You figure your major will come to you there. You'll have two years to figure out what you want to do with your life.

Now you may have been prepped by your school, or you may have to learn it on your own. You may be the first one in your family to have the opportunity to go to college. You figure that in your freshman and sophomore years, you can see what's on the buffet table of degrees and pick the one that lines up with your goals. Never mind the fact that you need to get scholarships and financial support to attend college or university. Also forget the fact that those two years of decision making are coming at a cost of $60,000-$100,000 per year. But never mind all that. You'll have your decision made by that time.

Then you hear about a graduate who spent four years in college, got a degree, and is now working in a field totally unrelated to their major. They're also now saddled with five and six figure debt. If only they had a transition year. If only they had a hallway to take the time to consider where their next steps would be. And that's the purpose of the hallway.

When you find yourself in a hallway, take your time. Choices made in haste instead of in a contemplative and pensive position may not be the best choices. Decisions made on emotion rather than logic already come at a disadvantage. They may be saddled with issues that need to be worked out had they not been made under those circumstances. It's important to take in your hallway moment to see what's being spoken to you and shown to you so you can decide on the next level.

Take note of the scenery in the hallway. Are there any tools or objects that will help you in your next level? Are there any people waiting in the hallway looking to couple up with someone who needs their particular skillset in that next room? These are vital questions to consider. The hallway is not just there for you to go through or simply a passageway where you can adjust your clothes and move through it. It should be seen as an opportunity to take a rest and take note of what you've taken inventory of that you brought with you, and what needs to be left in that area.

For example, if you come in from the rain and in the hallway is a place for your umbrella, you know that's where it would go. You don't want to drip water throughout the house so somebody could trip. Also, in certain homes, there may be a butler or a maid waiting in the hallway to show you to the office or room for you to make your appointment.

The hallway is as important if not more so than the doorway itself. The hallway gives you the opportunity to consider what you've been through and what you're about to go through. Some hallways are straightforward, meaning there are doors to the left and right. You need to know which doorway to select. Some hallways are still straightforward but have a door at either end. It's clear in those as to which way to go.

Now there are other hallways that are circular and encompass a building. Those hallways have doors around them and through them and some even lead to staircases. But your focus here is about doorways. In those circular hallways you have time to not only circumvent and see all your options but to pause and take into perspective the impact of each door. The doors may have signs on them that indicate what's behind them. Some doors may have a clear or frosted window. That means you need to read the sign to see what's behind them. If it's frosted or the blinds are down, then what's in there is only meant to be seen by those who enter and have access. If there's no sign or anything that's indicative of what's beyond that doorway, then you want to think twice before you put your hand on the knob or push and attempt to enter and what this could potentially cost you if it's not where you want to go. There's power in that hallway and it's up to you to figure out what it is and how you can use it effectively.

<u>QUESTIONS TO CONSIDER</u>
How are you using your time in the hallway?
Is it for recovery, re-focus, or refreshing?

Chapter Six:
Closing Doors

Give attention to what builds you up. Stop paying attention to what tears you down.

If you live in a cold climate and your winter is especially harsh, you'll long for the spring and summer months. That time allows you to be outside and enjoy the weather. You may also desire to invite the weather into your home. Now, the warm weather is a welcome visitor, and you leave the door open for it.

However, when that door is open, there's no one to see who goes in and out. In the summertime, mosquitos and flies are among the most unwelcome guests you can have inside your home. You probably get upset because you realize you, or someone else in your house, left the door open. You need to close the door or you'll literally become one with nature.

This also applies when you have an indoor kitten, puppy, or young children. As they get accustomed to their surroundings, they test boundaries to see how far they can go. The last thing you want to do is let them go outside by themselves where they could potentially get hurt. Which is why many parents' favorite question to each other is, "Did you close the door?" This includes cabinet doors, refrigerator doors, front doors, and any doors in your house.

As you can tell, this chapter is about closing doors, and I apply it to when you're reaching a goal. Your goal could be to change your mindset, to become healthier, to alter your surroundings, to transition to a new job, to get a promotion, or for higher learning opportunities.

Any of those could be your goal. First, you must take inventory, take stock of what's around you. Then, you have to see who's around you. We talk about opening doors, about going into the next level. However, what's also critical is closing doors. Closing doors is to make sure certain unwanted things don't get in. What do you want to close the door to in order to progress to your next level?

DOUBT

Why do you want to close the door to doubt? Doubt represents wavering back and forth between issues, an indecisiveness. This is an unwelcome trait when you're moving towards your goal. Doubt causes you to second guess yourself. It can create what's called analysis paralysis. You begin to scrutinize every move you make, every step, every thought. You hide behind the mask of "being meticulous," but it opens to a door to being in a motionless state. You don't move forward because you're stuck in various levels of examination. You don't move forward because you're scared to move, fearing you may have missed something in your first, second, or third round of checking.

FRUSTRATION

Oxford defines frustration as *"the feeling of being upset or annoyed, especially because of inability to change or achieve something."* It's a result of not knowing what to do in a situation. The inability you experience culminates in the prevention of progress. You make plans and you follow through with those plans. But something happens that throws you off track. Now, because you're not sure of your next steps, you become frustrated. This state also gives birth to feelings of stagnancy and immobility. Both of these are similar branches off the same tree.

LIMITING BELIEFS

Now, this topic can be a whole chapter in itself. Limiting beliefs are core thoughts that have become part of your value system. They could have emanated from societal challenges, familial struggles, environmental conditions, or institutional biases.

These thoughts keep you in a box, unable to move outside or beyond your self-made borders.

PAST TRADITIONS

Quick story. A mother was visiting her daughter and her family for the holidays. After playing with her grandchildren, she joined her daughter in the kitchen with her husband. As the daughter was preparing the ham for the stove, she cut off the ends of the ham before placing it in the pan. The husband asked his wife why she did that. Her response was that she saw her mother do it. When she asked her mom, the response was that she saw *her* mother do it. Later, when the daughter's grandparents came for dinner, they came into the kitchen to check on dinner. The daughter asked the grandmother why she cut off the ends of her ham before putting it in the pan for baking. Her response: "I cut the ends off the ham so it would fit into our baking pan."

That's a prime example of a past tradition that was passed down without explanation, just blind adherence. It's important to look at your actions and reactions to certain events and ask yourself the origin of the behaviors. If they're from past traditions, then you may need to retire them as they can prove to be unfit or even a detriment to your current reality.

YES MEN/YES WOMEN

These are people who think everything you come up is the best thing since sliced bread. Every idea you come up with is pure genius. They're not sure how they ever got through life without your input or ideas. Though their intentions are good, it actually becomes a hindrance to your growth. You're not operating in the reality of the situation when the feedback you're receiving is geared towards evoking a false sense of confidence and hope.

CONDESCENDING TALK

When it comes to condescending talk, you need to observe your environment. Be aware of who's around and what words are being used. Take into account what's being said around you, to you, and about you. Now, you can't control what's being said about you by everyone. However, you can control what's being said around you. Take note and relocate when necessary. Understand this, your surroundings have no filter. What's being said will operate and vibrate off what's around it. Be protective of it. Treat it like a newborn baby that needs constant care and attention. Just like a child or a pet, you work hard to make sure that it stays healthy and not exposed to toxic elements.

CONDESCENDING SELF-TALK

What you say to yourself trains your brain on what to attract and how to act. The limits you set for yourself are obviously self-imposed. Simply put, you need to speak yourself into a limitless life, one that's fitting your progression and looks to your future.

DISTRACTIONS

As innocent as they may seem, you have to become aware of what may be a distraction. There's a saying that says labels are for jars. The popularity of that phrase came during a time on our civilization when individualism and self-improvement became a movement of its own. People were tired of living and working under a pre-defined term or condition that emanated from prior condition or circumstance without their input. The premise of the quote, "Labels are for jars" is to make it clear that the definition of a person or the work they do came from them and no one else.

I beg to differ. When it comes time to focus, it's key that you become an expert in identifying and separating what helps you vs. what distracts you. Anything that draws your attention away from your intended goal could be termed a distraction. That could be a screaming child, social media, a phone call, texting, snacking, or TV news. Also, what may be a distraction one day may be a help the next day. It's about the timing and how the distraction may impact your progress to achieving your goals.

HOW TO CLOSE A DOOR

I've just covered a lot of what you want to close the door to. When you close a door, there's a process to it. Do you slam it shut or close it gently? When you slam a door, it sends a message that could be one of anger or of closure. It could indicate finality. However, if you're easing yourself into the next phase of life, then you may choose to gently close the door.

When it comes to people, you need to operate on a certain level of discernment here. Slamming doors may be received as rude. Your goal is not to burn bridges or tick people off. You want to learn how to back out and close the door on someone with a proper ending so you can get back to your progress.

Closing doors will become a vital part of protecting yourself and your goals. It's important that you correctly identify what's an obstacle and close the door to it. It's key that you realize not only what you open the door to but what you close the door to.

Make sure the door is fully closed. An example of not closing a door all the way is a refrigerator door.

Let's say you go to bed at 10 pm, but 8 pm was the last time you were in the fridge. You were sure you closed the door. However, the next morning, you walk into the kitchen at 8 am and the door is wide open. Immediately, a wave of emotions hit. They could be panic, anger, regret, or fear. Now, you have food to throw out, to re-stock the fridge, take time out to go shopping again, and spend money you didn't expect to. A potential day wasted.

The same applies to your goals. If you're closing the door to people, events, or other areas, make sure those doors are closed properly and securely. If the phone is a distraction, turn it off or put it in airplane mode while you work. If people are a distraction, go somewhere you won't be disturbed. If your room or home is distracting, book a room at your local library. There's an answer for your dilemma if you seek it out.

What you want to do is make sure you hit your goal, whatever it may be, so I hope this concept helps you. Remember, you may be good at opening doors, but remember to close those doors that don't support you so you can achieve your goals. What you have around you should push you forward rather than hold you back.

CLOSED DOOR = COMPLETION

A closed door represents the closure of a situation. Many times, you may go about your day, thinking you've finished with a situation. You need to realize there's a difference between finishing and completion. Let's talk about completion.

Say for instance you're in a conversation with someone over text. They ask if you want to meet somewhere. Your response is that you need to think about this and get back to them. Now you've had that conversation in the past. You ask somebody something, and they say, "Let me get back to you." But that never happens. What does happen is that the conversation is incomplete. There was no finality, no closure. Can you think back to times in your life when a conversation wasn't complete? What did you recall when you didn't complete something? That could have been a chore or an assignment or a conversation. You need to understand the difference between not finishing and incompletion or closure.

Closure is on the same level as completion. Completion is operating with a mature mindset. You don't go into a house and open doors, then leave either a back door or a front door open. That's incomplete, that's lack of closure. The same is true for thoughts and dreams. When you make a plan and act on it, you're now in motion. As you continue in motion, you see what you need to leave behind. You have phases in life where you start new areas and complete other areas.

You operate on a higher level of integrity as you progress on the path to your goal. An immature mind starts something but doesn't complete it. That's someone who will arrive at a destination and then worry that they forgot to close and lock their door. So, they spend the majority of time in worry and fear. They rob themselves of being in the moment. They've allowed themselves to operate in an incomplete manner, which leads to an incomplete life.

The lack of closure is indicative of deep-rooted issues that need to be addressed before true progress can be made. You'll continue to operate at a loss if you don't take the time to see where you have these open doors that need to be closed.

Consider this scenario. You're going on a road trip. You happen to wake up beyond the time you expected. Now you're rushing about to pack the car and get on the road at the appropriate time.

You may have a smart home, or an alarm system connected to your phone. But you're in so much of a rush, since you want to get out of the house and onto the highway. As you get on to the highway entrance, your phone goes off. You quickly look at your phone and it states there's a door that's unlocked. That unlocked door is preventing the entire alarm system from engaging.

Now you have a decision to make. Do you turn around and go back to the house to lock that door so the alarm system can be engaged? Or do you continue on your trip and hope nothing happens to your home?

Either way, your plans have been interrupted. This is the result of not dealing with deep-seated issues. This might be that you're not secure in yourself and are leaving the door open to anything that will keep you company.

It doesn't matter if it's something as simple as a road trip, a vacation, or a particular goal such as getting healthier or starting a business. Your habits are not discriminatory. They'll invade every area of your life if they go unchecked.

In certain buildings and places closed doors are necessary, such as a hospital or a doctor's office. It's necessary because of doctor-patient privileges. Also, it coincides with the protection and privacy of each individual and their medical condition. So, it's important that doors are closed and what goes on behind those doors are kept under wraps.

Another instance would be a police station. During any type of interview or questioning, police may use a closed door as a tactic to either get a response they need or instill a level of confidence and comfort to a victim relaying a story. Labs and medical facilities are also where closed doors are necessary to protect the outside world from the materials that are inside those rooms. Many times, we can understand the need for doors to be closed. It can be to either keep something in or to keep what's in protected from what's outside.

So, when you approach a door and it's closed, find out the reason instead of immediately attempting to open it. Think hard, observe the surroundings, and get insight into what your reasoning is for coming upon that door. Find out if it's locked, or if there's a security badge you need to get in. And is this something that may or may not have anything to do with your goals? If it's not in support of your goals, then going inside that room with the closed door would do more harm than good.

QUESTIONS TO CONSIDER
What doors have you left open in your life that need to be closed?
Are you operating in a state of non-closure or completion?

Chapter Seven:
Will Your Baggage Fit?

Live life like a doctor. Be surgical with your movements and operate in wisdom.

In my previous job where I traveled 50 to 75% of the time to train clients on software, my assignments covered 45 states and some international locations as well. I enjoyed the travel because it wasn't a hit and run, meaning I wasn't in one state for two days or another one state for one day. Anywhere I traveled, I was there for Sunday through Thursday or Friday. It gave me the opportunity to learn about that city, the roads, and the nuances of the citizens.

With so much travel, I had to become an expert with my baggage: bring what I needed and not what I didn't. Sadly, I was and still am a bit of an over-packer. I like to bring options. I thought I should be prepared for anything: formal, casual, or business casual.

But options take up space. Many times, I had trouble getting the luggage cart through the hotel room doorway. I often heard the question, "Is all that luggage for two people?" If the airplane weight limit was 50 pounds per bag, my bags would be at least 45 pounds. And coming back, I hoped I would get a kind check-in attendant who would look the other way if it was over by just a few pounds. That's when my sense of humor and hope of distraction would kick in. If not, my carry-ons were my back up for stuffing in clothes. Eventually I became better at packing. My goal is to avoid the embarrassment of re-packing my bags in front of everyone while holding up the line. And let's not talk about the food I would bring home. That's a chapter for another book.

When you're going through a door, sometimes you want to bring baggage with you. Let's define baggage in the literal term. This may include luggage, backpacks, suitcases, shopping bags, purses, satchels, or even a fanny pack. Now, what's the figurative definition of baggage when it comes to your goals? Old ways of thinking, overreacting, modeling your traditional thinking, and your traditional ways of taking action.

When you're approaching your door (your goal), you've already made the determination of whether it's a manual or automatic door. You have the right key. You made steps to gain the correct access and mindset for it. But there's one problem: the door seems too small.

For some reason, you can't fit yourself and your baggage through the doorway. As much as you make the effort and work to configure the bags, turning them around, or getting them at an angle, they can't fit through the doorway. Why? Because they're not supposed to go with you.

When we're talking about doors, we're talking about transitions, new levels, new rooms—whatever will help you hit your goals, arrive at your milestone, or meet or exceed your expectations. A key development in your progression to achieve your goal is finding out what CAN'T go with you. Remember this, what got you there may not be enough to get you to where you want to be.

The way you thought was fine got you up to that point. But now for you to transition to the next level, you have to adopt a new way of thinking. Your bags represent previous habits and items you've picked up along the way. They've served their purpose up to this point. However, if they're preventing you from going through the door onto your next stage, you'll have to make some hard decisions quickly. The choice is simple yet difficult. Either you leave some items behind and go through the doorway, or you stay in that room and hope you figure out a way to take it all with you.

BAGGAGE: TAKE IT ALL

Let's examine the latter option. Many people want to take it all with them. It can't only be habits, items, or feelings. "It" can also be people. That includes family, friends, distant relatives, colleagues, or acquaintances. You may want all of them to go with you to feel secure. They've been with you from day one, the start of your relationship, and you can't imagine going on without them.

This is where you want to work on expanding your thought process, altering your beliefs, and re-examining your core values to see what needs to be trimmed or removed for your breakthrough. You may need to get lean with yourself for your next phase. It's a cutting away process, similar to the pruning of a tree. Certain plants need to be cut to grow properly. Otherwise, they'll become disfigured and need to be removed entirely. You have to make that determination. Is what you're attempting to bring with you worth the risk of impacting your entire journey?

It may not be fun or pleasant but it's necessary. Bags are containers, holders of stuff. You need to examine every piece of luggage and its contents to see if they've reached or outlived their expiration date. Similar to cleaning the pantry and refrigerator, many people go through in the spring and fall months, they plan a day and go through everything in their kitchen to see what's expired and needs to be tossed. You do this to protect yourself and your family. There's a real danger to your health if you're ingesting expired food. The bacteria could cause short or long-term effects.

That's how you need to treat your baggage. Be mindful of oversized baggage that you're attempting to bring through a door. Don't force It. Don't break the wall. Don't resize the door. Don't bring tools out. It can't go through because it shouldn't go through.

Be ready to ask for help regarding this process. The friends, family, and/or coaches who work with you towards your goals can be a great source of insight regarding your baggage. They see your determination for achieving your goals and want to help you with sound advice to help shape your decisions.

Once your decision is made, be quick to execute it. Feel free to have a conversation. You're training your brain and your atmosphere for your next level. Look at that baggage and then say, "Sorry, you can't go with me. This is it. This is my new level."

RE-DEFINING BAGGAGE

Any time you hear the word baggage, your mind probably thinks of luggage, carry-ons, or garment bags. But as I've said before, baggage can also mean people. Some of the people "baggage" can refer to is family. There's a certain allegiance people have when it comes to family that can be termed either as a strength or a weakness. When you're growing up, depending upon the circumstances, many people develop a soft spot when it comes to their relatives and their challenges. It could be their parents, their siblings, or their cousins who could be around the corner or in another state.

However, we can develop a blind allegiance or preference when it comes to family. Also, we can be too forgiving when it comes to our blood relatives. Some family members have done grievous actions that have put them in a situation where they'll be behind bars. They may have stolen from you or done you a massive disservice. There are also instances of family members stealing IDs from other members in order to do illegal activities. Despite all of that, there are people who still give them a pass because they're related.

The challenge with having such a mindset is that it blinds you to what you need, and it can cost you serious delays in reaching your goals. People or friends can blind us to the help they might need, and we can assume we're the answer to the problems they have. But our goal is to not be a rescuer. We can provide help, but we can't presume we're the end result.

I had times when I had to learn to not be the rescuer. I had an instance where I was in a relationship with an individual who was on a higher level of access than me. We corresponded about restaurants, joked about food, and enjoyed meetings. So, when I saw there were people on their team who hadn't registered for a particular event, I took it upon myself to bring that to their attention. Instead of receiving the thank you I had envisioned, I received questions and puzzling statements about why I was even looking into their affairs. I even received a call about why I took the initiative to go that route. Thankfully, the person I received the call from was someone who knew my heart. Initially during our conversation, I was remorseful and apologized profusely about overstepping my bounds. I didn't want to be perceived as somebody who assumed they could take certain liberties just because of previous conversations.

However, after further discussion and thought, I became upset and disappointed. I realized it wasn't the person but my expectation that created my stress and disappointment. I realized then that I needed to step back and take inventory with who was with me and positioned for my next level. I'm grateful I went through that situation because it taught me to step back and think first before taking action. It also let me know that certain relationships can't go with me and aren't necessary for me to obtain my next level. More importantly, it taught me that I can't be everything to everyone, neither should I try to be. If I do, then I create that baggage and I can't fit it through the door.

Another reason to not be a rescuer is because you hide the true areas that need help. I have a friend who works for a non-profit organization. They have a couple of titles but mainly they're the go-to person when anything needs to get done. They handle scheduling, some contracts, equipment updates, appointments, and whatever the building needs and what people need. It's important to know that when that person is operating at full capacity those areas of lapse don't appear. The programs move without any flaws visible to the untrained eye.

Now if you sit down and ask that person what it took for this to come off and be as successful, they may let you in on all the happenings behind the scenes in order to stay on track. The good news is that the person will be taking a leave. That means all those areas that needed help won't get that support as it has in years past. Those areas will lapse, and it will stand out. This is good for leadership to see, because if something doesn't fail, then you don't know that it needs to be fixed. Bottom line, a rescuer has good intentions; however, it's a disservice if what they're doing is a patchwork job and what's needed is something more permanent.

The same could happen at work. You have someone who's a valuable employee. Some come in early and stay beyond their hours to make sure the work gets done. Though they're only down for 40 hours, they're nearly working twice that to make sure certain projects and deadlines are met. Everyone is familiar with how hard that person works, and some are even appreciative of it. Now the challenge comes when that person quits because they find something better outside the company. All that work that was done is left outstanding. It becomes a disservice for one person to do so much while others aren't being utilized. Or maybe everyone is working as hard as they can, but the project and deadlines are unreasonable with the current staffing. In those instances, it's necessary for deadlines to be missed and for projects to go on beyond their scope so leaders can see what's missing and address it on a more long-term basis.

Rescuers have good intentions, but the work that they do is a fallacy. It creates a false narrative that people operate on and become accustomed to. If management says they can get this work done and these projects accomplished with these numbers, then they move forward and present these numbers to the senior execs who make decisions and offers for new business assuming these numbers tell the true story. Since they don't, they wonder why goals aren't being met when they've committed to higher levels of production.

You don't need rescuers; you need temporary plugs until you can find a more permanent solution. It's the kid with his finger in the dike situation. He's smiling the whole time until he runs out of fingers and there are more holes to plug. That false narrative has long-standing implications that will ripple throughout an organization or through a person's life. Until they get down to the bottom of it, they will not realize that what they were given was not the entire picture. Making decisions on an imperfect picture can prove detrimental or fatal depending upon the scenario.

When it comes to your next transition in life, you need to be able to clearly define who and what can go with you. Does your baggage include past emotions and feelings? Are the people you're bringing along rescuers or encouragers? It's not about altering your vision. It's about seeing clearly and making the decision that may cause pain now but will be a benefit in the long run. You need to decide if you need to pack heavy so you can be prepared for whatever comes your way. Or do you travel light. The next move is on you.

QUESTIONS TO CONSIDER:
Have you taken the time to clearly assess the baggage you're carrying?
Who and what is necessary for you to go through the door to your next level?

Chapter Eight:
Fitting Through the Door

Motivation is for a moment; transformation is for a lifetime. Know the difference.

When a child grows comfortable with walking, they'll want to explore their independence. They mimic what they see. One way they do this is by attempting to open doors on their own. They stretch up to the doorknob, hoping they can reach it. As they continue to stretch, they now notice that the doorknob is starting to get lower and lower. In actuality, they're getting taller and gaining strength and knowledge with their motor skills. As they leave the house and begin to explore the world, they notice new and different doors. So, out of curiosity, they want to open these doors. Their fascination has been intrigued.

Doors come in different shapes and sizes. A child can learn this quickly as they may have a toy house that has a door. They can easily open that and slide toys inside. The child knows it can't fit through the door because it's not made for them.

Some doors are massive where you can just walk through them and bring whatever you want with you.

This could be anything from garage doors to car dealership showcase doors to movie studio doors. I used to wonder how those cars got into the showroom of a dealership, so clean and immaculate. I then realized it also depends on what door I'm going through.

So, there may be times where you need to be sure if you can fit through the door. It may seem like an odd question to ask yourself, but it bears merit. If you're carrying too much "emotional" baggage, in the metaphoric sense, you may not fit through the door.

Ever see a toddler dressed to their eyeballs for winter? It's very cute and hilarious. Their arms are extended out and they're waddling from place to place. The hood is tied on and the mittens are fastened to the coat for safe-keeping and loss prevention. Parents know the time that it took to get them all set, which is why they keep asking, "Do you need to go to the bathroom?" They realize that with all those clothes on, an emergency bathroom break becomes a hindrance that may have some serious repercussions later.

The same happens as we attempt to go through our doorway to break through to the next level. Maybe there's something you're wearing that's preventing your passage. It could be something on your back (a backpack full of emotional baggage) that's causing you to not fit. You want to squeeze your way through. You want to edge your way through. What are you wearing? What do you have on? What's preventing you from transitioning to the next level? Consider your clothing, what you "put on." as your attitude and mindset. Let's think about this. It could be:

PROCRASTINATION

This could be a heavy winter coat with a massive hood, a large zipper, and tons of buttons. Procrastination is such a huge weight to carry. It's detrimental to your development and can cause you to miss opportunities. Those who suffer from procrastination wait until the last minute to get anything done. Then it becomes a mad scramble to reach the deadline. That last day can be one of regret as you think over all the ways you could have used your time better. Regret does nothing but sap your energy if you let it. That's not a place you'll survive or thrive if you choose to stay there.

SELF-SABOTAGE

This is an offshoot of procrastination. You pack too much into your day. You have every hour planned. You go from zero to 60 without thinking back to when you had difficulty shifting from park to drive. That's an example of self-sabotage. Another is over-promising yourself or your services in a verbal or written contract. Because your desire to be part of something overwhelmed your logic and time in the hallway, you now have periods of anxiety to meet a demand that shouldn't have been yours in the first place. These are what could be limiting you from being able to progress to the new level.

DOUBT

If you're doubting yourself, that's going to prevent you from going through that doorway. When you question yourself, you get stuck without moving forward. It's called "paralysis analysis." I mentioned this concept in an earlier chapter.

NEGATIVE SELF-TALK

Understand that most of what we say to ourselves is negative. We don't necessarily say those thoughts out loud.

So, are you wearing any of the above items? Is that something you think you need to bring with you to this new level? If so, they may be keeping you from going into your next stage in life. You're transitioning to frustration and procrastination rather than the next step in your path. Bad habits like grabbing fast food, staying up late, or not being able to manage your time will weigh you down and hold you back.

A lot of items can go on that list—items you're wearing or ones you're carrying. These bad habits are on your back, and they've been a part of you for a long time, like another limb or appendage.

So, if you've been wondering why you can't fit through the door, it could be because what you're carrying isn't supposed to go with you! When you're transitioning to a new level, it's time for you to get lean. It's time for you to get crisp and precise with your thoughts and your movements. You do this so you can shed what's holding you back.

When you transition to the next stage, you can meet or exceed your expectations. When you're held accountable, you can say, "This didn't go with me. I came in crisp. I came in focused. The only thing that came with me was a new mindset and the ability to fit through the door." Know what you need to do to fit through that door. Then you can transition to your higher level. Whatever the milestone is, shed what you don't need so you can move through and succeed.

YOUR CURRENT FITTING

Today because people are living longer, a lot more options exist for eating healthier than there were 50 years ago. Entire stores and companies are dedicated to the advancement of a clean lifestyle that includes food and our way of life. Today, we have the most gyms and fitness centers in a square mile radius. Back in our parents' time, you could only go to a gym during working hours and rarely in the evening. Now, you can go any time of day, 24/7.

Those of the millions who are always dieting mostly focus on food and exercise and use both to get healthier. But food and exercise are only part of the picture. If you're at a size that's unhealthy for you, look at your lifestyle. Examine the habits that got you where you are. When you discover the source, you can work on changing the habits that will pervade throughout your life if you don't make the proper lifestyle changes.

Therefore, it's not a nutrition or exercise change that will get you to your goal. It's about changing your perspective. Once you adapt the most effective mindset, you strip away what's holding you back. Your goal is to become "lean" and I'm not talking about your body. You need to get lean with healthy habits, so you have what you need to fit through the door to the next level. As you stay focused on your goals, the superfluous actions and thoughts in your personal and professional life will stand out that much more. You can now work on removing them so they don't become a hindrance in reaching your next milestone.

Live life like a doctor. Be surgical with your movements and operate in wisdom.

I used this quote in an earlier chapter. Now the example I'm giving in this quote is that of a doctor. If you were born in a hospital, then a doctor is the first person you meet. Many people relate to doctors because we consult with them whenever we have a health issue that needs attention. We do our research and go to the proper doctor who specializes in that area. Doctors have high levels of education, having studied for years. They go through rigorous trials in their residency and in their practice. Of course, there are not only medical doctors but different forms of doctors such as doctorates in science fields, education, business, and psychology.

Any time you hear the word surgery, you know this is a high-level medical procedure involving insurance companies and various opinions, consultations, and thought processes. Depending upon the surgery, this may involve one or more specialists. Also, based on the medical need, the surgery may need to be done in two or more different parts based on the healing required. Surgery involves precise movements that take planning.

The patient is aware of the doctor visits and consultations. What they don't see is the planning behind the scenes. The blueprint that's designed, the plans that are made, the discussions that are had between various offices to ensure that the surgery goes off well. Most times, you get the opportunity to set a date for a surgery that's far ahead. This gives you time to prepare yourself physically and mentally. If it's an emergency, then it needs to be done right away.

By being surgical with your movements, you're analyzing each scenario and moving methodically. This is not paralysis of analysis. This is walking forward with both eyes open and with a high degree of awareness. This is a higher level of thinking, a deeper level of processing. Not only are your moves more precise, but it's also knowing the degree of leverage you have for making mistakes. Surgeries aren't the epitome of perfection, but they come as close to ideal as possible. These should be the types of movements you want to make when you're progressing your actions towards a milestone that helps you achieve your goal.

There's a difference between knowledge and wisdom. *Knowledge* is obtaining information about a particular subject. It's the gathering, collecting, and reviewing of materials that pertain to your goals. *Wisdom* is knowing how and when to apply the knowledge you gathered. In short, knowledge is the what and wisdom is the how. I could have easily said to move in wisdom. But when you hear the word operate, it connotes a more detailed degree of movement. There's more weight to the word operate. Ask any patient listening to a doctor give a recommendation. There's a difference between the word procedure and the word operation.

Though I'm an only child, I come from a big family. I have nine uncles and aunts in total. Except for one, we all live in the same state. And we all keep in touch, visit, and stay within a short driving distance of each other. My grandmother came from a family of 13 siblings all in the same household from the same set of parents. They were living in the south in the US and back when having a large family was the norm. Everyone looked out for each other and everyone knew everyone's business. If you got in trouble at school, you would hear about it all the way home. All the neighbors would make sure to give you the insight and their hindsight on what you did wrong and how you better not do it again.

That feeling of camaraderie was prevalent because we knew we had a struggle and commonality. That common struggle is what brought us together to celebrate the fact that we made it this far and to realize the potential on how far we could go. We also got together to remember those who have passed on and celebrate their memories. We would laugh and joke and have contests about who could tell the best story. That's how we celebrated and enjoyed each other.

There was time for the kids to play games together, compare schools closed, and share friendship. As well there was time for adults to get together and talk about their families, jobs, neighbors, and any gossip. And of course, there was church to discuss which had its own section for comedies or sad stories. All of this was intertwined in the fabric of life. No one was left out except for one time when the day turned into night or when some of the other relatives showed up. These were the ones who brought adult beverages as well as adult language and adult stories. They carried a spirit that permeated the air. Even children could tell that the atmosphere had shifted. It was at this time that the grown-ups were separated from the little ones who would either go to bed or to a section of the house where they would continue to play.

THE SHIFT IN FITTING

When it comes to going to new levels, you need to gain an understanding that what got you here isn't enough to get you to the next level. Your previous understanding is what got you here. This current level is designed for you to use your past, learn from your present, and use that to step into your future. Your mind must go through a change. You have to wrap your hands around your value system, pull it up from the roots, and throw it away. What I mean is this. Your belief system is deeply rooted in your psyche. It defines the way you move and process events and emotions. In order for you to proceed, you can't cut and properly remove what you can't see. Why? Because the root remains and can grow back. You have pull it up and make sure no remnants are left behind to grow.

You have to become a new source. Before you unplug, you need to see what's feeding you, what gives you that energy. What's the action that's going to give you that next break, that's going to give you that vibration, that's going to link you to that next level of operation? When you determine how you'll structure yourself, then it becomes an opportunity and a place to develop a basis for operating on higher levels.

Your goal is waiting for you to come through the door and grab it by both ends. It's not waiting for you to struggle with, to talk it from a ledge, or talk it down from a tree. Your goal is something that's been crafted and patiently waiting for you since it began as an embryo in the back of your mind. It's been something that's been evolving through the years, with the patience of a doctor doing an 11-hour surgery on three hours of sleep attempting to operate at the optimal level. What's different is that you've been sleeping for years.

When you wake up it's now a new day. A new dawn. A new season. Let old ways die because they won't fit into what you have that's new. You've outgrown your old ways, and it's not even comfortable for you to walk around because they don't fit you anymore. Growth requires new clothing. Old clothes get ripped and frayed and are not able to stand up to the trials of this new level. They were made for a period in time. You would be ignorant to continue to put them on and care for them as if they had longevity.

If the clothes you put on communicate that you have a higher understanding and that they operate at a new level, it's time for you to resonate this fact and operate accordingly or be uncomfortable through the next phases of your life. It's not a difficult decision, but it is a decision you need to make. What are you going to do with the door in front of you? How are you going to handle the door that awaits you? Will this be a milestone you reach or a millstone you allow to hold you back or weigh you down?

This is where you disconnect from your past beliefs and traditions. Traditions are what you learn from and not necessarily the next step forward. Make sure they don't hold you back or keep you in the place of "close, but not there yet." Be willing and eager to exchange your old ideas for new ones. It's better to talk someone from an old chair to a new chair if they're already standing. Meaning if someone has preconceived notions about a certain subject, it's better if they're in a position to exchange them for new ideas vs. convincing them to abandon their beliefs. Save your energy for convincing yourself and use that as the catalyst to push through the door. Sometimes it needs to be a forceful shift. But do what's needed to make sure you come through it successfully and are obtaining your goal with new confidence.

Here's the challenge. You're trying to fit in somewhere you belong or should I say don't belong. You may need to contort yourself to a point where you're not comfortable and that by the time you go through that door you're bruised and banged up. There could be some broken bones, roughed up skin, or dislocated ligaments that occur because you're eager and pressed to go through a door that's not made for you. Now the question becomes: how do you want to appear when you go through this doorway?

This chapter is called Fitting Through the Door and you want to find one that was made for you. If this is the door you're going through, there shouldn't be any harm that will keep you from going through it. You could be hurt on one side of the doorway but through the experience from the previous stage, you're being shaped into the position needed to handle what's on the other side of that door.

I'm sure you've seen TV shows and movies where someone wanted to escape but got stuck trying to fit through an entrance that clearly wasn't made for them. They were either too big or were carrying too much. Either way they didn't fit. Maybe they had to remove some article of clothing they were wearing. Maybe they had to remove what they were holding in order to make it through. They had to either decide whether to risk their lives to go back and reach what they couldn't bring or move forward. They hoped to obtain what was originally in that grasp. By the way, it makes you wonder what would cause a person to wedge themselves in that doorway. Fitting in the doorway shouldn't be the issue unless it's about what you shouldn't be bringing into your next level of achievement. If you have nothing in your hand and you still can't fit, then you have to see what you're holding on to mentally that could be the trigger or indicator that you're not to bring it. Or is this door the one you should be going through?

The purpose of seeing if you're the right fit is about you having what it takes to handle the next step. Are you bringing what you need with you? If it's a wide door, should you be bringing more with you? Just because it will fit through the door doesn't mean it should come with you.

QUESTIONS TO CONSIDER
Have you removed all non-essentials so you can fit through the door?
Is there something you need to let go of to move forward?

Chapter Nine:
Who Has Access?

*What you can hear can define your day, so guard
your ears and listen to wisdom.*

When I was in middle school, I was learning
about parties and dances. Dances at school were for
celebrating a particular time of year: Homecoming,
Spring Term, or Prom. Parties are events around the
neighborhood, at a residence, hall, or park. This
usually involves a birthday party, baby shower,
confirmation, graduation, or quinceañera.

When I learned about neighborhood parties, I
decided I wanted to go. I would make the effort of
taking the train downtown, meeting with my friends,
and going shopping for our outfits. We would spend
hours matching clothes, trying them on, getting the
right cologne or oils needed. However, what I
quickly discovered is that I can't just show up to a
party. Either I had to know someone there, or I had
to arrive with someone who had access to let me in,
in other words, was invited. It's horrible to prepare,
get friends, and arrive at an event only to be turned
away. The difference between these events is not just
the theme but who has access to them.

Who has access to go through the doorway into your next level? Now, this might seem cruel but hear me out. Certain people are in the room with you now. They could be family, friends, colleagues, co-workers, networkers, or acquaintances. These people could have been a help to get you to where you are now. They've been your cheerleaders and encouragers constantly exhorting you as went from trial to trial, or room to room.

Others may just be along for the ride. They haven't harmed you by contributing to your negative self-talk. But they haven't been much of a help, either. They could be watching your progress and decide to hitch themselves to your wagon, in hopes of achieving similar successes.

However, when you transition, when you walk through a door, it's important to see who has access to your next level. You've got to be able to look at people and ask, "Are you pushing for me to go forward, or do you want me to stay here?" You need to do this if you want to reach a milestone or to improve your life as you reach for your goal.

You may be saying to yourself, "I want to get to a position where I can write a book. I want to start a business. I want to be promoted to this next level so I can manage more people, make more money, have greater influence. Where can I grow mentally?

Maybe I can teach, motivate, or learn a new language. I can imagine going beyond where I've been." You have to be able to see who's with you pushing you forward or who wants you to stay where you are.

Those who want you to stay here are not necessarily bad. Sometimes you may want to put them in a mental box. You may think they're terrible for you. No, keeping you from moving forward doesn't make them a terrible person. It doesn't mean they don't want your best intentions to materialize. They're still there for you. They still care for you. However, the challenge is that you can't transition to the next level with them. As we learned in a previous chapter, you have to gently close the door on them.

This is vital in your progression to reach your goals. You may not like the idea, but it is necessary for you and for them. If you can't shut them out of your life temporarily while you progress, you may grow to resent them. Once you realize what you're giving up in order to maintain the relationship, negative feelings could creep up and poison your thoughts. You may begin to blame them where blame is not warranted.

But they aren't to blame. They just don't have the perspective you have. You need to make the decision to not take them with you and follow through with it. That's not to say there are those who can tell you they're not coming along as you progress. Those people have been through experiences and have learned to discern when they should or should not be in someone's life. But those people are few and far between. Don't let this fact exempt you from being able to make the decision to move forward with or without those people.

There's a saying that says "labels are for jars.: The gist of it is that everyone is unique and can't be put into a box or category or label. I understand the importance of that. Oh, how times have changed. I think that it's more necessary when somebody is operating with a lack of knowledge vs. those using labels for the purpose of identifying and categorizing. Regardless of what you may want to think, labels are used all the time to define people and demographics. Take voting as an example: Democrat or Republican? Labels are also used to define particular groups as in technical groups or in hospital settings. Though the saying has some relevance, it's not a blanket phrase. If you've ever filled out a job application online, you know the "voluntary" section very well. Those questions are asked for the sole purpose of categorizing or "labeling" your application.

ACCESS USING MATHEMATICS

For further clarity about those who should or should not have access with you as you move to the next stage toward your goals, I like to use the mathematical terms of addition, subtraction, multiplication, and division.

Let's start with addition. Some people in your life are there to add to your life. Now just because they're additions doesn't mean that what they're adding is going to be a benefit to you. And when you initially hear the term addition, it sounds like something that's going to be positive, that someone will add value to you. However, someone could be adding their drama to your drama and that doesn't do you any good. So, it's important to make sure you define those who are additions are truly adding value.

Next, we have subtraction. Some folks are looking to subtract from your life. That could be what you have to offer your local community or the world. Just because a person is a subtraction that's not necessarily a negative connotation. If someone is here to take from you whatever is a burden, then they're there to lighten your load. Ask anyone in a staff call center about the need for addition and subtraction. Anyone who's well trained to handle the calls coming into the center is an addition that has a significant subtraction of worry and busyness that was previously part of the template of the call center.

In other words, more people mean they can handle the queue. However, if those people aren't properly trained, then they'll add more work behind the scenes to follow up because of poor or inadequate training at the beginning. So, those people you identify as subtracting from your life should be there only if they're removing obstacles meant to delay you and not to progress you.

Next, we have our good friend multiplication. You probably know people who are looking to take what you have and multiply it, so it has a compound interest for you to achieve your goals. Now those are the people you want to focus on and make sure you have them around and that they have access to you. Those people are looking to multiply solutions vs. multiply problems.

The last term is division. I'm sure there are options where division can be used as a positive. However, for the sake of this example, I'm using it as a negative. Those who may be around you could be seeking to cause division in your ranks. They want to get close to you, to see who has your ear, and plant seeds of divisiveness and contention. Those are people who masquerade as plants looking to beautify your garden but in reality, they're weeds. They choke the life out of anything that hopes to bloom. You need to know when to remove them from your environment.

I like this parable in the Bible that talks about a man who owned a field. He had workers in his field who tended the plants. At night some thieves came in and planted weeds among his plantings. When it was discovered that there were weeds growing, one of the head servants went to the master and stated that a thief must have come in during the night and planted these weeds. The intention of the thief was to confuse and be a hindrance to the owner of the field so he would give up and lose money.

However, when the servant asked the master if they should remove the weeds, he responded that they should hold off for they could uproot the proper plants before their time period. The master had the wisdom to give the instruction to allow the weeds to grow along with the wheat until the point of maturity. At that time, it would be more discerning for the servants to distinguish the weeds from the wheat.

So, there will be a time when you recognize that some people in your life may wish to do you harm. However, to remove them initially would be more of a disservice then a service to you. There are times where you need for them to grow together with those who are there to help you so their real intentions are recognized, and then they can be removed. They won't be removed by your actions but by their own hand. Their actions, their comments, their words will be tell-tale signs to those around them that they don't belong, and they'll be removed by the community members who are there for your upliftment.

What it all comes down to is this. You have to treat your journey like a temple. It has a sacredness to you that some, a few, or just you understand. Though someone or something is well intended, does not mean that access should be granted. When you get over the fact that denial to you is for the benefit of others, then your decision making becomes clear. You begin to see things for the long-term and realize that a little pain now and better than a living a later life of regret and misery. Watch who has access and how much.

QUESTIONS TO CONSIDER
Have you made a list of who has access to you, when, and how long?
Does your environment add to or take away from your progress?

Chapter Ten:
Walk or Run

You don't need to stand OUT to be outSTANDING.

When a baby is born, the first type of movement they can do is sit up. Some babies may start with rolling over or lifting their neck. None of these is insignificant by any stretch of the imagination. But for the purpose of this chapter, we'll focus on sitting up.

Once that child learns to sit up, they'll want to move from one point to another. All babies start off with a crawl, some crawling backwards. I'm not sure what that's about because I haven't done the research. However, it's an interesting phenomenon and warrants further discussion. After a child learns to stand, they're ready to walk. They learn to balance themselves and walk forward as they've seen others do around them. Depending on the environment, the child may walk first and no longer desire to crawl. They may not want to be held anymore. They just want the awesomeness of being able to walk and move on their own.

Once that's been mastered comes the running. And when you run all out, you have no concern about how you look or how much energy you need to expend to get from one point to another. As you get older you become concerned with how you can get somewhere more efficiently and effectively and you learn to pace yourself. You're also concerned about what you look like when you run. Whether it's societal or familiarity, you dig into your running style. You look at different shoe and clothing styles, where to run, when to go. You decide if you're running for health or competition. Are you running to catch a bus, a taxi, or are you late for work? Each phase of life dictates your movement and whether you decide to follow that or go against the grain.

So now I need to ask: will you walk through the door to your goals, or will you run? As you're transitioning from one level to the next, as you're going through the next doorway—whether you're going into a hallway or to another room—you have to decide if this is something you can walk through or something you need to run through. And what's the difference between the two ways?

WALKING

As you're walking through, you're able to take your time. You're making sure whatever you need is coming with you and whatever you don't need is staying. You know you're progressing. You understand you're taking this transition. You're making notes. You're saying, "This is my next level. This is where I need to go. This is the step I need to take. This is why I need to go to meet my next goal. This is what I need to do to be a better me."

It could be a team or could be a new people. New actions, new habits, new lifestyles, all of what you have to take into consideration. You have to be open for this. So, as you're walking through, you're observing your transition. You're transitioning from the old place to this new place.

Another benefit of walking is the additional perspective you gain from it. I was in a predicament once where I was required to walk to regain my strength. So, rather than drive around my neighborhood, I walked. As I took these walks, I was surprised at what was around me. I noticed who takes care of their yard, if someone had a front yard or back yard, and if they had a pool or pets. Along the way, I also met my neighbors, some for the first time since I moved there. You can only meet so many people if you're driving. But walking affords you the opportunity to have a conversation, learn who's in your neighborhood, and what their interests are.

Though I didn't have a pet, I was still able to appreciate the benefits that walking gave me.

When you walk through your doorway, take some time to look around. Focus on what's there, what's coming with you, and what you're leaving behind. In the process of walking, you develop an appreciation for where you've been and where you're going. Your mind is afforded the opportunity to settle into this new mindset.

RUNNING

Now that you've seen the benefits of walking, let's discuss running. Sometimes you may need to run through a doorway. Why? Because what you left behind in the previous room may hold you back. It may even be chasing after you. It wants you to stay. So, sometimes it's necessary to make a hasty departure. You'll want to run through the exit so your unwanted baggage doesn't come with you. Or before anyone notices you're gone. In the short-term, this may seem harsh but better for you in the long run. (Pun intended.)

I live in an area where I see lots of walkers and joggers. I'm working on being a constant walker. Emphasis on the word "working." However, I have friends who are joggers or runners. I'm amazed at their stamina, running for periods of time up and down hills or on just on a straight pathway. So much goes into running and I get exhausted just watching those who run. Did they take a running course? What got them into running? What do they do to prep themselves before they run? Did they start off running one mile at a time? Do they run on dirt or cement? Is there a difference? What type of diet and exercise would I need to follow to get myself up to being a runner? Do I even want to be one? What I do know is that they're running as I'm walking, so they'll get to their destination quicker than I will. I often wonder what destination they're going to. Are they running to a specific location or are they running for their health?

Running comes with its own sort of prep. Some people run in pants, some in shorts, some with a heavy shirt, and some with a T-shirt. Some people run on tracks vs. the open road and some prefer a dirt trail. When done properly, running can be a benefit to one's health. However, if not managed properly, running can cause injuries that can be either short or long term. You might think that if you find yourself running, you may be running out of fear. Perhaps you feel you need to escape something and you're afraid what's chasing you may catch up to you.

Let's lay that to rest. When you're running through a doorway, you're moving quickly with determination. You know where you want to go. You've worked hard to obtain the focus, discipline, and training to get there. You hear the starting pistol and take off. There's a big difference between running with fear versus running with confidence.

Now, what could you be running from? People, old habits, procrastination, poor time management, binging on social media? Not having the proper balance so you're living a healthier lifestyle? Having that lifestyle means that you're operating on all 10s, to be able to advance to your next level.

TO WALK OR RUN

As for whether to walk or run, just know that sometimes there's a need for you to run through that doorway. Also, remember to shut that door so what's trying to come after stays in that room. As you're going through the doorway, grab the doorknob and pull it tight.

It's up to you to decide if you need to walk or run through the door. Walking might be necessary but running may be critical. Just know the difference between the two and make your decision.

When you choose to go for a walk, there's much to consider such as what the purpose is. Are you walking to enjoy the weather? Or perhaps for a change of perspective? Many businesspeople will opt to walk when they're working on a project. Science has shown that certain chemicals are released that help generate new ideas and a different perspective when you change environments.

Are you going out to get a breath of fresh air and relieve yourself of some stress? Being in a closed environment all day can be a challenge. It's important to go out, inhale fresh air, and release any tension you're experiencing.

Are you walking for the purpose of exercise to stay in good health? When you walk, you want to consider the weather. Is it raining, snowing, or sunny? And where do you want to walk? How long do you want to be out? What will you wear when you're out walking? A lot to consider before you even step out the door. So, when it comes to your next step or your next milestone for your goals, you can see how detailed you need to think and what you need to consider so you can be prepared to walk that walk.

That's how much walking plays a part in your progression in life. It's methodical, calculated, and planned. It also allows for proper course correction if an unexpected event happens. Weather-wise, if it's raining, you may need to find a gym or an indoor mall where you can do your walking. Same thing in life. If you're ready to walk through a door and an object falls in front of it, you'll have to plan how to deal with it. Step over it, go around it, move it yourself, or get help. But this is all based on taking the time to step back, take inventory, make a plan, and execute on that.

Now, if you're running, you have a shorter timeframe to adjust. There's still time to correct your course, but you're moving at a faster rate.

Another question to consider: Are you running towards something or from something? This decision will determine your stance, sight, and body movements. And your mind has to process this new information. Whether you're running towards your goals or away from them, the connotation is up to you based on the subject you're discussing that relates to your goals or the object that your progress attracts. Just because the word choice has changed doesn't automatically make it negative or positive. It's how you frame it, how you position yourself, and how it ties into your goal.

Running towards something is usually positive such as a finish line or a marker along the way. You get a sense of accomplishment. However, if it's something you felt you should already have and is slipping away, then you're in a state of playing catch up.

Your mental health plays a part in the achievement of your goals. Your dreams and goals are important parts of your well-being. Psychologists will tell you that the achievement or the lack thereof a person's goal can have a physical impact on the body and of course the mind.

This isn't about paralysis analysis. You don't need to examine everything to the point that you won't make a move at all and you stay stuck where you started. You just want to do the due diligence you need to examine those around you and the actions you're about to take to make sure they align with your goal. Then go through the doorway by walking or by running—your choice!

QUESTIONS TO CONSIDER
Have you thoroughly defined your reason for walking/running through the doorway?
Have you outlined the pros and cons of choosing one over the other?

Chapter Eleven:
Screen Door or Solid Door

In all things, make sure you FAITH is bigger than your fear.

I won't make the generalization that every person loves summer. But it is an enjoyable time of year. After being cooped up in the house for the previous few months, you get to go outside and enjoy the sunshine and wear short sleeve shirts and flipflops. You want to let the air in. Now, it's time to put the screen door on and enjoy the fresh air coming into your house. Prior to that, the door kept you and your family separated from the elements. You felt protected knowing that what was outside was not getting inside.

What type of door are you dealing with for your next level? Is it a solid door or a screen door? We'll talk about the screen door first.

SCREEN DOOR

You're approaching your next level. Through a screen door, you can see what's next as you continue on your journey. You have time to prepare yourself. You know what the appropriate clothing is for the next steps. You can also determine what bags, if any, need to come with you, such as mental baggage, emotions, past traumas, and experiences. Having a screen door with the ability to see what's on the other side can be a good or a bad situation. When you're able to see your next level, then you can either run to it with enthusiasm or choose not to. This is what you've been working for, so you'll want to make the step to your next milestone.

However, there is a flip side. Seeing what's next may cause you to be apprehensive about what your next phase is. This could be starting a business, wanting to be healthier, or learning how to de-stress yourself. It could be learning something new such as an instrument or a language. It could be goals like a promotion or a higher degree of learning.

When you have a screen door, you can see there are pros and cons. You know it can make you run to it or make you pause. Why? Because you feel you may not be ready. Now, this can turn into an opportunity to see areas of yourself that need attention. What's causing you to hesitate? Take time to source that feeling to see where it comes from. This time of introspection may prove crucial and beneficial in your breakthrough process.

SOLID DOOR

With a solid door, you can't see what's on the other side. Screen doors give you that benefit of seeing and preparing. But there's a different mindset when dealing with a solid door. Here's the situation. You're preparing to leave the room you're in to ascend to that next level. You know where you want to go and what the next steps are. You've created a plan and have been following it from milestone to milestone.

With a solid door, you're operating strictly on faith. As stated in the Bible, "Faith is the substance of things hoped for, the evidence of things not seen." You're opening that door, or the doors are opening for you. You're walking through with everything you can take or nothing at all. You're just walking through pure and clean, anticipating what's to come and ready for anything.

So, you never know what that next level will be. Sometimes you can see it, sometimes it's just a matter of walking through by faith. In your mind, you have a vision of your destination. And then there's the reality of it. These may be dueling concepts.

I've been a fan of words ever since I was young. I like the way they describe objects and how they can be used to influence. By the switch of a letter or an emphasis on a different syllable, you can conjure up

124

feelings in someone such as inspiring or discouraging them. Whether a person was a poet, a speaker, or a mathematician, it didn't matter. If somebody could twist a phrase to get their point across, they had me hooked.

I also developed a love for studying the mind and how it's able to form and transform one's environment. I read these stories about people who were in extreme weather but not impacted simply by sheer will. It's similar to the magician who walks over hot coals in bare feet. It seems to be mind over matter. So, when I see that someone's mindset can be impacted by a twist of words, I'm immediately attracted.

I also love to motivate and help people transform. It gives me a thrill to plant an image in someone's head and have them break through their barriers. For example, I recently developed a saying that I posted on my various social media platforms: "Fast your fears and feast your faith."

SCREEN OR SOLID: FASTING

Assuming that not everyone is familiar with the term "fast" let me give a brief description. A fast is a period of time when a person restrains from food to focus on a particular purpose or goal. I became familiar with the term from the Bible. Growing up going to church, I was accustomed to the New Year's Day fast. This is where we fast for the first few weeks of the year to consecrate the rest of the year. You must get your doctor's okay before fasting for lengthy periods of time.

I wasn't a fan of fasting. I was a fan of feasting. And just by one letter, you can see the difference between the two. I like to eat whenever I like to eat. For me to be on a fast had to be for a special reason.

But I digress. Fasting in the way I'm using means to restrain from nourishment. Feasting means the opposite. Many of my readers, followers, and connections know the difference between fear and faith. Fear is what holds you back from what you desire to do. Faith gives you the inner strength to step out, uncertain whether or not there's a step in front of you that will support you.

Imagine that these two are inside you: fear and faith. Every day they're battling to govern your actions and thoughts. Throughout the day they're constantly warring with each other to see who will take supremacy, who will be on the throne of your life for that minute or day.

Imagine they're pets. Now both need nourishment to grow. In the fight, whoever's the strongest will win. You can clearly see that whoever is better nourished will come out on top. So that's why I encourage you to "fast your fears and feast your faith."

Realize that both need nourishment to survive. Yet, they live on separate food options. Your faith needs to be fed with constant food, that is, positive thoughts. What you see, what you hear, and what you say are what feed your faith. Your faith is discerning, so it needs to be intentionally feasted. Whereas your fear will eat anything. It doesn't matter whether it was nourished properly or is in an emaciated state, it will eat indiscriminately. Additionally, your fears will grow bigger with silence, idleness, or procrastination, which is like a main course for your fears.

So, picture yourself as a chef. Every day you need to prepare the right meal. If you don't prepare the right meal, that's still a meal. And your faith and fear will eat from the same plate. The question is are you providing what will feast your faith and fast your fear?

That's the key difference between the screen and solid door, the latter of which represents faith. You have to look at it as if you've already spoken and lived in what's behind it. Between the solid door and the screen door, which represents fear, one is not better than the other. It's knowing when you encounter them, how to handle them.

Now a screen door may be deceptive because it can cause you to pause when you should be going through. The danger in seeing what's on the other side is that your sight becomes the antagonist to your vision of what you want in life. It's key that as you progress toward your goals, going from breakdown to breakthrough, you need to operate in a larger understanding that what you see doesn't correlate to what you imagine. Vision and sight operate on the opposite ends of each other. It's important to note that sight can become an enemy of vision, especially since it can ensnare and paralyze you at your point of breakthrough.

There's a biblical scripture in First Corinthians that says faith comes by hearing, here and by the word of God. Now utilizing this with what we've learned so far, in order to develop your faith, you need to speak to it. If your faith has a particular diet and that diet is comprised of certain words and phrases, then you need to speak those words that will build up your faith. Understand that faith is what you need to reach your goals. There's nothing unintentional or deliberate that won't be an aid or a detriment to you. Whether you're active or passive, faith will feed off both. It depends on what's in front of it that will nourish or decimate it. As you walk forward and through to your door, be cognizant of what you say or what you hear that can impact your faith and your progress towards your goals.

I previously mentioned that having a screen door allows fresh air in. You also have to consider what is allowed to go out as well. When you have a screen door vs. a solid door, there's another level to understand and appreciate in knowing the difference between the two. It's easier for words and sounds to go through a screen door than a solid one. For instance, if you live in a neighborhood that has cars going by playing loud music or making noise from a loud muffler, those noises will be a nuisance if not being met by a solid door. Sure, a screen door is great at letting in air but not so great when it's letting in noise like unwanted music, firecrackers, or barking dogs. Believe me, I speak from experience.

But what if you have no screen? No barrier means everything is allowed and without any filter. This includes flies, mosquitoes, and other insects. Anything that creeps and crawls looking for shelter and a place for constant food and water will be attracted to your home. Also, whatever weather is happening outside can come in as well, such as rain, sleet, or hail. So, screen doors and solid doors indicate a certain level of filtering that's needed when it comes to the achievement of your goals. Not everything can be let in, nor should it be. Also, you want to be mindful of what you let out. Not everything you speak or discuss is for public consumption. Some words need to be kept in secret until the time for revelation. Your next step in your journey in life can either be a solid door or a screen door. The decision you make is either based on what you see or the level of your faith and preparation. You could be going into a room or a phase in life that has you handling more than you have ever done before in your life. It's unfamiliar. You need to decide will you succumb to fear of the unknown because you cannot see the next step, i.e., a solid door. Will you fall victim to fear of known BECAUSE of what you see i.e., a screen door. Regardless of what you're dealing with in front of you, it's how you build yourself up that will have you walk through the doorway with confidence.

QUESTIONS TO CONSIDER
What steps are you taking to starve your fear and feed your faith?
Have you prepared yourself for each door when you encounter it?

Chapter Twelve:
Equipped for the Door

If you STAY ready, you don't have to GET ready.

When you're young and just learning to walk, you want to go everywhere—indoors, outdoors, in malls, and to stores. You're in your discovery mode. The places you're most familiar with are your crib and your bedroom. As you get older, your senses get more acute. Your brain starts to develop and desires for more knowledge and input. You're still mastering your native language, but you hear things that pique your curiosity. Your parents come in and out of your room with new and different stimulants for you. It's only natural for you to wonder where they go and how you can get there.

So, you start off the crawl. Building up muscle in your arms and legs, you balance yourself and attempt to move forward. Now, we have need to get introduced to our friend called coordination. From the parent's perspective, it's intriguing to see a child learn how to move forward. Some of them start going backwards. Others may drag themselves forward. But the determination is still there. As you get closer to that next room, you get excited because you're about to make a new discovery.

However, there are still some doors you may not go through because you're not equipped. As a baby, everything is bigger than you. The good thing is that you have no qualms, hang-ups, or fears about asking for help or using whatever is close to get to where you want to go. I've visited friends who had a child just learning to stand. It didn't matter that they had never seen me before. They wanted to stand and saw me as a useful tool to get them from their crawling position to a standing position. I love the fact that kids will do that with no fears, no compunctions. In their mind, they see a leg, and they grab it and use it to pull themselves up. Then they look at you as if to say, "Thanks," and then move on to their next challenge.

As a small child, a door may be too big for you. You're not equipped for the door because you haven't gained the right height, muscle, or technique to open that door. As much as you desire to speed up the process, it still takes time. Now, what will actually enhance the time are 2 issues: diligence and consistency. If the child truly desires to open a door, they'll continue at it whenever they can. When they're awake, when they're playing, while they eat. It's a constant fixture.

The same concept can apply to your goals. What steps are you taking to equip yourself to open that door to your next level? Understand that there may be a cost for you to get that knowledge, obtain that understanding, utilize that wisdom. It may be a one-time fee or a monthly subscription. It will also require that you make sacrifices with your time. That includes social, down-time, bedtime, and more. Yes, the cost is real. The question you have to ask is how much more is it costing you NOT to take action to equip yourself for that door.

PROPER EQUIPPING

Some parents know they have children that have advanced beyond their previous preparations. They've purchased child locks for their kitchen and bathroom cabinets. After a period of time, this child gains the knowledge on how to open those cabinet doors. I've seen so many videos of children inside refrigerators who have ransacked snacks because they broke through that door. The children at some point became equipped to get through that door.

Are you technically equipped to handle the door? If you remember when you were in school, you learned how to escape a fire. When I was in school, we had a fireman come to our school and teach us about this. If you're ever in a building or someplace that's on fire, you should stop, drop, and move to the best opening.

Also, before you leave the room, you should test the door. You touch the door and notice how it feels to you. If it's hot, you don't want to open it. Why? Because you don't know what's behind the door. Whatever it is, you're not equipped to handle it. Don't go through. You're trapped. You don't have the equipment to handle what's behind that door.

It's the same in life. You need to know what's behind the next door. When you touch the door, what does it feel like? Does it feel hot? Does it feel cold? Does it feel some other way that doesn't feel normal to you? However, it feels, you have to ask yourself if you're equipped to handle that door.

If you're not, then you may need to do something from where you are in your current situation that will equip you to handle the door. Also, you may need to wait for someone to come through and assist you or provide you with the right tools to handle it. It's not so much just about going through the door but being able to handle it and seeing how it is. You want to allow time to pass so you don't harm yourself on the burning hot door handle. You don't want to be ill-equipped when going through a doorway.

So, apply this to life goals. Your goal could be getting healthier, starting a business, getting a job, obtaining a higher degree, learning a language or an instrument. It could be an internal discipline or feeling better about yourself. Maybe your goal is to experience more joy or to operate on a higher level.

When you watch sports, you'll see particular players who start and some who come off the bench. Other players don't come off the bench for some time. They may not play games on a consistent basis. However, whether they're playing in the next game or three games from now, there's an expectation for them to be ready at all times. So those bench players don't practice just before the game they play. They practice as if they're playing in every game. They know that their preparation can be a key factor in the team's progress throughout the season. Their diligence shows the coach that they're a viable option if a starting player goes down or is unable to play.

If you stay ready, you don't have to get ready. What that means is that when the time comes for you to walk through a door to your next level, you'll be ready, you'll be equipped. The difference between getting ready and being ready is about operating with a different mindset so your present is always operating in your future.

Here's a scenario I think you can relate to. If you're going to dinner and need to leave the house at 9:00 pm, you don't start getting ready at 9:00 pm You're ready by 8:00 pm and positioned to exit and be on time. The same is true in your progression to your goals. You need to prepare yourself for what's going to come that ties you into your breakthrough. Just because you can't see it in the present doesn't mean you can't envision it. You want to know what you need to be ready for the opening of the next door. When you shop for groceries, you're more efficient if you prepare a list instead of going up and down every aisle to remember what you need. It's better to come equipped than not equipped.

Staying ready means being mindful of what's around you and making sure it's still current to helping you when your level arrives. As an example, when doing maintenance on your car, you want to stay on top of the regular schedule so a light doesn't come on your dash indicating engine problems. And with your goals, you want to be up to date and aware of the current state of affairs and potential future for where your goal may take you. That way you stay ready when the time comes rather than getting ready when it arrives. This readiness is what equips you to go through doors.

QUESTIONS TO CONSIDER

Have you measured the cost of not taking action? What price do you have to pay in dollars and time to move to your next level?

Chapter Thirteen:
Crossing the Threshold

What you can hear can define your day, so guard your ears and listen to wisdom.

Throughout the last 12 chapters, we've been talking about doors and doorways. I encourage you to please go back and do yourself a favor. Read all the chapters as there's a progression. I associate doorways with progressions or going to the next level.

I want to explain the importance of crossing over the threshold, that piece in the doorway that separates one room from another. It could be a piece of rubber or metal. It's the line you cross between transitioning from one room to the next, from one level to the next, from one milestone to the next.

A progression is involved when you cross the threshold. It's an important milestone. It's significant in your journey. It doesn't matter what your journey is, there are no limits. You've now made steps to achieve the goal you set when you began this journey.

Along the way, when you transition from one step to the next, you cross over a threshold. This is a borderline that signifies the completion of one level and the progression to another. It's a moment of celebration. It's a moment to note in your journal. You'll want to look back and see where you've come from as well as where you're going. As you cross the threshold, you step over and into your next place on your journey to your goal.

Whether you run over it, step over it, or walk over it, it's still a crossing. So, know the significance of the change when you cross thresholds into new levels. Now, not everybody you know can go with you. Not everything you have can go with you. Just know that it's the closest step to your next progression, your next milestone.

To reach your goal, the threshold you're crossing could be the last threshold you cross. You could be in the completion phase of your goal. You've taken your main goal or vision and broken it up into milestones. Then you've achieved enough milestones, so you now have the foundation. You're about to lay the final piece on the building that's now connected to that threshold. So, wherever you are in life, please note the significance of the thresholds as you cross the doorway.

Here's an example of what I mean. In a race with about 30 to 40 million contestants, only one will win the prize. The starting gun goes off and off they go.

They're competing for one main prize. It's anybody's game, but the strongest usually wins this race. After a lot of twists and turns, the winner reaches the mark. What happens after that is a period where they're growing, developing beyond where they were when they first arrived. During that time, the race host is going through changes as well. They begin to mark each time they hit a milestone. In the beginning, it was a wonder that they even reached the milestone. to both the winner and the host. As the time drew closer and closer to the finish line, both became anxious. They were excited and more than ready for this next phase to come. When that day finally arrived, the host and the winner crossed the same threshold. We all know this threshold as birth.

Every expectant mother will tell you that they live in anticipation of this crossing. This is one of the ultimate thresholds. It's a changing of the guard. It's new life and growth into an unknown world where dependence is the key factor. It may seem dramatic, but every living being is familiar with the concept of birth.

Here we want to revisit the power of a proposition. Many schools have cross country teams and running coaches. They teach you style and technique as you run to optimize your ability. When it comes to crossing the finish line, they don't tell you to run to the finish line. They tell you to run through it. The reason they do that is because many people will start to let up on their speed as they come up to that ribbon. To prevent that from happening, the coaches will tell the runners to envision themselves running THROUGH the finish line and to a point past that. They know they not only need to work on the physical aspect but also the mental aspect of running and completing, of crossing over that threshold.

THRESHOLD RE-DEFINITION

A threshold can also be defined as the magnitude or intensity that must be exceeded for a certain reaction, phenomenon, result, or condition to occur. I'm a fan of spy and action movies so I'm familiar with this. Many times, the protagonist is stuck somewhere and he has to make a decision to push the vehicle he's in and/or the room he's trapped in beyond the threshold in order to save the day. The threshold is there to show what the limit is or the capacity of the container of the materials. Materials refers to the mental tools you picked and are using to move to your next level.

Usually in movies it's nuclear or radioactive. When the meter of the machine measuring the capacity goes beyond the safe zone, then it's time for an escape. In this context I'm using the term threshold as a line that needs to be crossed to begin a new phase. You hear someone saying that they're on the threshold of their career which means they're in a new world, a starting phase that will launch them into a new era and environment.

Something I learned while writing this book is that it's essential to have a goal beyond what you want. If you're looking to lose 10 pounds to be healthier and fit into a different outfit, my suggestion would be to set your goal to lose 20 pounds. What happens is that you trick the mind into aiming far beyond the limit. When we know what a limit is and we often aim for just that point.

Years ago, I worked in a call center. I was trained for four weeks and then had to pass a test in order to keep the position. I needed to take the Series 6 Exam, a regulatory test, so I could discuss with and assist clients on life insurance policies that had transfer ability, known as variable life policies. Within these policies, a person could do a dollar transfer from a from a small cap account fund to a large cap account fund, for example. To be able to do that and to be in compliance with state and federal regulations, I had to study and pass a test.

Something we were told as we were studying was that we had to get at least a 70% to pass the test.

That's where the training team dropped the ball. Many people were still studying so they could get a good enough grade to keep the job. When you're studying with the mindset of being just good enough, you're already working with limited abilities. You've told your brain it doesn't have to operate on full capacity. It follows instructions and only gives you what you need for that moment. It's up to you to bring out anything else you need after you've set the parameters of insight and understanding to be available to you for this job.

I have some close friends I made during the training who didn't make it through to keep their position. Thankfully, one friend found another role within the company after he made a successful argument of the monetary investment the company made in training him. Only now do I realize that if they had set the bar higher, they would have gotten more for their money. More of their trainees would have passed the Series 6 and be fit to fill the positions.

When you set the bar so low saying this is all you need to pass, then you allow people to do the bare minimum. You need to realize that whatever position you're in, you set a standard. If your standard is just barely passing, that's going to be the results you'll get. When you're setting up yourself for success, you need to push beyond the measured and common factors of success. You need to move that threshold to a point where you're moving beyond it vs. going just to it.

THRESHOLD AS A STANDARD

The next phase of life you're going into is not a stopping point. It should be seen as an area where you're learning and developing to get yourself closer to and beyond your goals. That area will train you and equip you with the skills necessary to handle the obstacles and challenges that go with that phase of life. It could be a sharpening stone or the potter's wheel shaping you in the mold you need to fit for that next door. A key example is how swords are made.

Swords are first seen as metal that's beaten into a specific shape. It goes through pounding and breaking for the shape to come forward. Afterward, the sword is then thrust into the fire and pulled out a total of seven times. Each time the fire is made that much hotter. The purpose is for purification. There's a combination of beating with the hammer and sticking it into the fire so the best metal can be formed in this manner. The goal of the fire and the hammer is to rule out all the impurities that would weaken the metal during a combat or a fight. The sword has crossed the threshold from being a hunk of metal to a weapon of offense.

Every summer in the US, we hear about forest fires that devastate acres of forest. People have lost homes and are displaced because of these massive disasters. However, what we don't hear about are the deliberate fires that are set to purify the land. Fire can destroy brush lands, but the ashes help make the land productive. Many people see fire as a transformer of the negative to the positive. It's a revealer. Fire removes the dross, or waste of a thing; it exposes the elements that can weaken and pollute.

Fire is used to burn up all the elements that would cause a sword to be anything but strong. That's why it was put in the fire at least seven times. The goal was by that last time the only thing left would be pure and could be used as a true offensive and defensive weapon.

Fire is also considered a pure element of nature because it never becomes polluted or impure. All the other elements can be depleted or removed by human action. But fire can't be tainted in any manner. It's useful in that it shapes objects so what's left can be of use. Now you can cross over to the next stage as you cross over the threshold because what's left after the fire is useful, rather than weakened with waste.

We can't forget about the hammer and the important shaping of the sword. What the hammer does is beat and shape the sword, so it's used for the purpose for which it's made. The fire may remove the impurity, but the hammer gives it shape. It's no good if the sword is pure but the shape is ineffective.

We need to realize that we're being shaped and formed to make it to and through the threshold. The next level we're going into is what will define us and have us be of use when we're in our community that meets the need of our gifts. The skillset we've shaped, the timing, what we have to offer is vital as it gives life and purpose to what it's connected to.

So, the threshold is not just for you and it's not just an end point. It's the beginning and a large marking of an achievement done and a path well worn.

QUESTIONS TO CONSIDER
Are you working towards your goals or beyond them?
How can you use your threshold to push beyond your limits?

Chapter Fourteen:
What's Blocking Your Door?

Let your dreams be your source, not your goal.

What's blocking your door? The scenario we're going to use is moving. Let's say you've been living in a house. You have a couch, a loveseat, or a sectional. There are closets you haven't been in. You're coming to an apartment. As you're looking around, you might see a door or a closet that doesn't seem to be in use. You want to open it. You see the doorknob. You want to pull on it. However, something is blocking it. It might be a table, a couch, or some type of furniture blocking it. It's an obstacle preventing you from opening it.

In the US, the South has many large homes called plantation houses. The intention when they were built was to house large families with enough space for everyone to move around and live comfortably. Also, they were built with the intention of housing other family members or friends who were visitors for a period of time. Back then, it was a journey to visit a neighbor as the houses were spread far apart. If someone traveled hours to come visit, hospitality would dictate that you offer them a room

147

to stay for the night. So, homes had to be built to accommodate that.

Many of these homes had rooms and closets that weren't used. The family might use them for storage, but that was it. One option would be to fill up the room with furniture and place it in front of the closet. This was done more for an aesthetic appeal. Over time, this became customary as a decoration. If a closet wasn't in use, putting furniture in front of it showed that it was blocked off and no longer of use as it was originally intended.

So, when you look at this from the figurative sense now, what's blocking you from opening your door and preventing you from advancing to your next level. What are you looking for? What is it that's blocking your door? What's keeping you from going to the next level? Is it your current environment where you live?

When I pose this last question, I'm not referring to a physical location. I'm referring to mindset. Do you live in doubt? Do you live in frustration? Do you live in fear? Do you live in low self-esteem? These are beliefs and feelings that may be blocking your door and you can't see them. Sometimes we make these issues so big, we can't see the doorknob in front of the door. We can't even see any way to access it. Our vision becomes delayed or denied by what we see through our mindset. Still, we know there's a door, yet it seems unable to be opened.

Could it be people blocking your door, people in your life who have now reached the end of a season? There's a saying that people are in your life for one of three purposes: a reason, a season, or a lifetime. You have to find out what's blocking your door. You need to determine what's preventing you from opening and going through to your next level or transition.

Once you uncover your block, you can take steps to move it out of the way. You might need help in moving it if it's a big piece of furniture. You may need to move a little at a time. That could look like changing your beliefs or your perspective. It doesn't happen overnight, especially when it comes to your core beliefs.

You also may need to stretch before moving that item in front of your door. By stretching I mean moving beyond your limiting thoughts, going beyond your sightline, stretching your faith so it's ready to move your blockage.

BLOCK EXAMPLE

Here's an example about a young man named Jack who has aspirations of being a musician. So, he invests his money in purchasing all the right

149

instruments. He even goes as far as purchasing videos and books to train him on becoming a top musician. Jack does this over the course of two to three decades. In the meantime, he goes to school. He graduates and gets a job. He hangs out with his friends and goes out to movies. He spends time going to parties and buying clothes. But he hasn't practiced the instruments. He hasn't put to use any of the materials he purchased in all those years. So, what's blocking Jack from becoming the musician and living the life he desired?

Jack had good intentions. He bought the equipment and had everything he needed to be a musician. He has friends who are top of the line musicians working in their field. Jack has access to all one would think he needs with the door right in front of him. Why can't he walk through it? Because something is blocking his door. For Jack, what's blocking his door is procrastination. Jack has all the outside trappings, but he hasn't committed the time and practice to attain that level of mastery when it comes to his music.

I bet you can relate to Jack. There may be something you've been dealing with since you were young that's been blocking your path to realizing your dream. That could be low self-esteem, lack of support, lack of confidence, feelings of not enough, or other false beliefs. However, if you don't deal with those blocks, they'll continue to stop you in your quest for achievement. You won't be living the life you want to live.

If what's blocking you happened in your youth, can you still overcome whatever happened many years later. After so much time passing, can healing still have an impact on your life? Yes, it can, for the remainder of it. You may require more healing to overcome any issues or circumstances that arose over the years since the original situation that created your block. Having matters block your door means they also attract other blocks to make it that much bigger. So, it not only blocks your door, it blocks your vision of it. You can become so engrossed in the issue itself that you forget about what's behind the door which is your passageway to the next level in your life. As I mentioned before, don't look at the problem, look past the problem.

How do you deal with a huge matter or a series of issues that are blocking your door? You take one step at a time to decipher what you need to do to remove your block. What's the issue? What's the source? Can you handle this on your own or do you need help? You may or may not require outside intervention. Imagine you're moving from one residence to another. Some boxes you can just grab quickly and move out of the way. With others you need to bend at the knees and brace yourself because the box is full. You don't want to pull a muscle moving this box out of the way. If you had smaller items, you might be able to handle them two at a time. If a sofa needs to be moved, you need someone to assist you. This is the idea of a helpmate.

HELP WITH THE BLOCKAGE

The term helpmate is a biblical term initially introduced in the book of Genesis. Adam was first created and named the animals. Though all the creatures had themselves, there wasn't one comparable to man. Thus, Eve was created.

Now when you're thinking about a helpmate, you want someone who has comparable strength as you so they're able to help you in your task. The person who's helping should be at least equal to you or have areas of strength where you're weak so you can balance each other out.

If you need help removing your block, get somebody with greater strength who can compensate areas where you lack. They can be someone who's been where you are and has learned how to overcome their own blocks successfully. I add the word successfully because anyone can overcome a block, but you want to gain victory by getting more out of it than when you started. That's one of the main differences between victory and triumph. Victory means you just won. Triumph means you won and came out better than where you were when you started.

The clearest example I have was when I was listening to a teaching where the trainer stated that if you need someone to help you lift a couch, you're not going to get a child. You would get somebody equal to you who can help you move. It can be someone who is equal to or has greater strength than you. Either way the job gets accomplished.

ADDITIONAL BLOCKAGES

Blockages are created when there's an outstanding issue that hasn't been dealt with either mentally or physically. There are those who've had a heart attack or some type of heart issue and need a bypass to remove a blockage. This blockage may stem from genetics or a poor diet and lack of exercise. Those who are diagnosed with coronary artery disease have a narrowing or blockage of coronary arteries, usually due to plaque buildup. Blockages are caused by the buildup of cholesterol, fat, and other substances in the heart. It takes time for this to build up. The body is made to heal itself and fights to stay healthy. Regardless of what you eat or do, the body is designed to function in a certain manner provided it has the right materials being supplied regularly.

It's the same when accomplishing your goal. You need to pay attention to any red flags as you go along your journey. Examine them and make sure you're aware of signs of blockages. The earlier they're caught, the earlier they can be removed. But as time goes on and the blockage builds up, it's that much more of a process to remove it on your own, possibly will need a specialist. You have to look at your supply to see what's feeding that blockage. What are you allowing in that's giving life and power to the block?

You want to be intentional when you identify your fears and the supply lines feeding them. Cut them off so they remain small and unobtrusive. Next, you want to redirect your supply line to your faith. Your faith is what fuels your energy and your goal achievement as you work from it. You want to work *from* your goals not *towards* them. When you work from them, you'll seek only those people who are aligned with and have their same goal of manifestation as you do.

To redirect your supply lines, take a look at what's feeding your block, in other words your fear. It may be necessary to not just cut it off but to examine the materials going in that built up any fears that were blocking and preventing you from going through your door. See, it's not just a matter of redirection but also inspection. Your faith won't grow if it's got bad supply lines or if you don't have the right materials, the mind-set, and the right team around you to build you up. Your faith doesn't just grow on whatever you give it. But know this: your faith is only as good as what you're feeding it.

You may have fears and past problems that are blocking the doorway. The first step is identifying them. The second is defining them thoroughly. The third is to come up with a plan to deal with them. The last step is to execute on your plan. Leave room for external help, but the catalyst for action is developing yourself internally. Your mind must be set on wrestling with the problems until they're removed from the doorway. Then you can walk through successfully, knowing that the problem is defeated and you have emerged victorious and triumphant.

QUESTIONS TO CONSIDER
Is there something in your life that you thought was a help but is an actual block?
What steps will you take to clear the path for your progress?

Chapter Fifteen:
Partial Door Opening

Feedback is only good if you use it to feed forward.

When I was young, my family had many get-togethers. We enjoyed each other's company. The adults and children shared the same space. That was until nighttime. Then the kids had to go into another room. It was time for us to go to bed. That's when the real party started. Now, if I wanted to see what was going on, I had to go to the door and crack it. Through that partial opening, I would hope and pray that I'd see something juicy.

Nothing really exciting ever happened, but sometimes I'd catch a glimpse of a card game, or some dancing. The most I would get was a partial look through a partial door opening—and not the full story.

What's preventing you from opening the door all the way? Imagine you see the door. You know it's time for you to transition from one level to another. Maybe you're being promoted. You're advancing. You're going further in life. Whether it's with your health, work, business, or some type of self-improvement program. Perhaps you're doing something on your own or with someone else.

Now, you have to go through the door. Maybe you've had this instance when you're trying to open a door but it's not opening all the way. You've got to give it more strength. What's preventing that door from opening all the way?

When you're in an apartment or a house, you may try to open a door, but there are boxes against it. So, you have to squeeze past them to get in. This represents something in your life such as bad habits, anxiety, or self-doubt where you're not trying to eliminate them all the way. You only want to deal with a part of them so you can get to the door. Imagine trying to sweep a floor without moving the furniture. You're only going to get a partial cleaning rather than a thorough cleaning. Doing something partially is not progress. It's not the step forward you need to take.

Take a look around to see what must be completely gone, what must be eliminated from you and the area so you can open the door unhindered and progress to your next level. What's preventing that? What have you not completely eliminated?

You might feel you can handle a little now and deal with the majority of it later. What you're dealing with can be on the mental (self-doubt, low-self-esteem), physical (poor shape), spiritual (hopeless), or emotional (depressed) plain, and those need to be eliminated. They impact the livelihood of other people as well. Those are the hindrances as you're trying to get through this door.

When you came up with your goal and the milestones to achieve it, they weren't partial in your thoughts or speech. They were complete ideas. However, they're preventing that door from opening. You can open it by a crack but trying to squeeze in isn't going to work. You don't accomplish your goals for that stage in your life, so you can't progress through the door. It's a requirement you need to meet to continue on.

PARTIAL BENEFITS

There is, however, a benefit to having a partial door opening. Many times, we look for what will inspire and push us forward, an accelerator. What will start a fire in us that will blaze and give us the momentum we need to push that door wide open. If we look around and don't see anything, it can easily discourage us. If we're in a room that represents a particular stage towards your goals, and we feel we're alone, then we can look inward rather than outward for inspiration. Even the word inspiration has an inner connotation. It means to fill with an urge to do something, especially something creative. So those definitions come into play when we're looking outside for something to light a fire on the inside.

What some people don't realize is that what was external was connecting with something internal but dormant. It's the Law of Attraction being put into practice. Any thing, person, or circumstance surrounding you is attracted to what's inside of you. We see that now with the use of online advertisements. If you visit a shopping site and purchase an item, you'll begin to see advertisements for that same product on the side or the bottom of another site you're browsing. That is just a programmer using the Law of Attraction by generating code that mimics this on a virtual scale.

Now back to our partial door opening. When you have a quick view of what your next level is, it can speak to what's already inside you and be the catalyst you're looking for. For example, if you're an athlete and you're vying for a position on the team, you may be able to see specific techniques and attributes that are required in future team members to execute their plays and take them to a championship level. That inside information gives you a push to not only adjust your preparation but to be more precise in your movements. Simply stated, you have the inside track on being the next most valuable player depending upon what you do with the information. So let that partial door opening be that spark you need. Allow it to light the fuse so when it comes to the end of it, you're off and running through that door which is no longer partially but fully open to you.

One saying I've been keen on is this. Feedback is only good if it helps you to feed forward. It's the same quote that's at the beginning of this chapter. When you think about feedback, many people brace themselves mentally, some physically as well. Sometimes it has negative connotations, so the person has to steel themselves to prepare for it. Other times, feedback can be done in a positive light. The person providing the feedback wants to provide constructive criticism to help the person move forward.

There are many books that you could place under the category of constructive criticism. The goal of the author is to give a response and provide a way forward for the reader. Now, the person receiving the feedback has a choice. They can either act on it or not. But it would be foolish of them to continue to solicit feedback from various people and groups and not move on it. Instead of acting on it, the person becomes more of a collector of wise counsel. He becomes a hoarder of wisdom and knowledge but not a user or purveyor of it. The contention I have is that you want to ask for feedback for the purpose of moving forward. That could be on a project, a goal, an assignment or whatever the case may be. But if the intention is not to move forward, then there's no need to solicit council. There's no need to send out emails, ask questions, or put together focus groups if you don't use the information accurately or ever.

Many times, we fight, argue, and struggle because we do not understand the whole point and can see the picture in its entirety. Because of past experience, a partial opening is viewed as a disadvantage and denial of access what we see as rightfully ours. Yet, if we step back and realize the gift of what we see and how much we see, we can take that into account and make necessary adjustments to move forward. We come to the understanding that the partial view is an upgrade from no view and are grateful for what we see. Take a moment and celebrate your view of the next phase in your life.

QUESTIONS TO CONSIDER
Are you dealing with a partial opening or partial viewing for your next goal?
What steps are you taking to apply with you see in your part viewing?

Chapter Sixteen:
Door Hinges

May your light shine bright so others can shine with you.

Certain doors need hinges to open them. I say certain doors because not all doors require them. Sliding doors for examples are on a track. They move back and forth either manually or automatically.

Hinges allow the door to open and close, and the handle is what unlocks and locks the door. However, the hinge plays a vital role in the proper functioning of it. Now we're talking about manual doors that operate by hand. Many of those doors have three hinges: one for the top, one for the bottom, and one for the middle. When it comes to your next phase, you want to know what hinge will help you turn the door. Sometimes a small hinge can turn a big door.

For example, you may need to make a small deposit to gain access to a PhD program. That small amount is now opening the door for higher learning. That higher learning in turn will open doors to new levels and new access. You'll then be able to exchange old ideas for new ideas. Also, this will allow you to expand your container, your brain capacity and intelligence. It's critical to where you're going since you can't put new ideas into old frames or the sides will break. The new program you're walking into will then allow you to expand your sides as you progress into new levels of learning. It's vital that you come into the full knowledge and understanding needed for you to operationalize your movements in this next phase of your life. You're becoming more present to the mindset required that will help you take full advantage and maximize the tools before you.

Another hinge could be a gym deposit so you can travel the road to a healthier lifestyle. See, the deposit is minimal but what you have access to will cause you to develop new ways of thinking and add to your desire to explore avenues you couldn't see unless that deposit was made. You now have access to different equipment and instructors who have knowledge and can introduce you to options of exercise that don't enter your current frame of vision. Also, your sight can now match your vision as you see those around you who have taken the journey and have reached a milestone where their external becomes a catalyst to their internal thus pushing them forward in their path to a new lifestyle. You start to see six packs and eight packs, toned muscles, people putting in work to get to their goals. You have now entered a community of like-minded individuals who've cultivated an atmosphere that will help propel you forward.

All this was accomplished with a small hinge. So now you can understand the power of a hinge and that it helps to open the door leading you to a milestone that traverses your ultimate expectation. This particular hinge was vital and continues to play a part because it's the opening and lever that moves your mind and being to new plateaus.

You may be familiar with the movie *The Titanic*. Here was a case where the engines were moving at a fast pace propelling a massive load forward. When the iceberg was spotted this became a massive challenge. The goal was to change the course of a huge vehicle with too small of a rudder. Another problem was that the lookouts didn't have the proper tools to distinguish objects in the fog to prevent catastrophes. You can see how the proper tools are necessary to plan accordingly when obstacles present themselves and you're given enough time to make adjustments that will cause small delays but won't abort the mission.

Ask yourself what it will cost you if by looking through the partial door opening you do nothing. How much money will you lose? How much time will be lost? It's not only what you have access to and what you say but how you use and employ that information.

Glimpses are given to those who know how to use that information effectively to get ahead and help those around them. This partial opening can be seen as an optimistic viewpoint. Partial means that the door is on its way to being opened or closed. But the fact that it's in between two states now presents an element of choice. Someone or something left the door partially open or partially closed. This is now your opportunity to take advantage of the situation and move to a position of acceleration and advancement. While the partial door is not closed, look and see what's inside. You can then determine if you're ready to cross that threshold and go in there fully. The glimpse in itself is a hinge that causes a change in trajectory regarding your goals.

You might realize that the hinge in the door is part of a larger structure. When a building is constructed, the foundation is laid first. Without a solid foundation the rest of the building would crumble when it's being tested by the elements. It's important to know the structure of the room or building you're going into. What's the foundation it was built on?

In life you'll come up against your own elements and you need to be sure you can weather them. If you build your house on sand, you know it'll fall when the first windstorm hits. However, if it's built on stone and reinforced and fortified, the house will last for many years and will provide protection for those in it. A house that isn't built on a solid foundation will be a danger to those in and around it. When you decide to make a house your home you must do the due diligence to avoid putting yourself and those you invite in your house in danger. Once the foundation is laid and the structure is built, the doors are important for you to take advantage of what's inside. So, it's key to examine the structure to see if it's viable for your next move.

Will the structure be able to hold what you bring to the table? If you have a large family and you move into a one-bedroom, one-bath house, then there will be limitations to work and live with for it to be considered a safe house.

This is why it's important to examine a structure before going through the door. You may be eager to cross the threshold but realize what it entails. You need to develop an understanding that just because the door is partially open doesn't mean you have to walk through it. Open doors don't always mean it's an invitation to come in. Open doors can be scenario for danger or a trap. If a door is open, you need to ask yourself why. Is there something in there I need to get and come out with? Is there something in there that could do damage to me and anybody with me? What are the indicators outside that door to let me know that what's inside is beneficial for me?

Size doesn't matter when it comes to your next phase in life. Whether the hinge can fit in the palm of your hand or is the size of basketball, you now understand that the importance of it is your preparation for next phase that opens up. You have the opportunity to take into account your current state and company and make the necessary choices that help you reach that milestone towards your goals. The choices you make and continue to make will have an exponential impact as you continue your journey. Don't discount the small decision until you can determine the magnitude of its effect.

QUESTIONS TO CONSIDER
What small moves can you make that will have big impacts in your progress?
Has the understanding of the hinge changed your views of your goals?

Chapter Seventeen:
Summary

Now it's time to move forward, for you to make a move and go through the door. My intention is for this book to serve as an opening for you to discover dormant skills inside you and the triggers needed to activate them. Your goal is to use them to achieve and surpass your intended goals. I want you to win. You want to win. And those times when you don't win, you can choose to look at the experience as a lesson where you learn and prepare for the next time you come upon this obstacle.

Something inside you was attracted to this title. As you perused the table of contents thoughts began to spark and connect. From the title to the chapters to the summary you're reading now, all this has been a doorway and threshold you've been preparing for. Though you may not have realized it, you've been on a journey that's taken you through each step. Little did you know as you began to read this, that you gave me permission to use the wording and the scenarios in this book to take you on a journey of self-discovery and insight. You allowed me to be your inner tour guide. Anytime I'm training and teaching, I remind those listening that I'm not teaching you anything new. I'm just reminding you of what you already know. What I'm doing is reshaping and redefining tools that have been before you but were not initially seen by you as being relevant to your goals.

Though you may not have paid much attention to them before this, doors and doorways will now take on a whole new concept to you. Whether you're going through an automatic or manual door. Whether you're going through a closed door where you need a security badge to gain access. When you reach for your keys to get into your house, the ideas in this book will come to mind.

My intention is to change the landscape of your horizon so your sky is just a limit, and you move beyond that vertical movement. Being stuck is no longer in your vocabulary because you now have the tools to look at each obstacle and see it not as being stuck but as a learning opportunity.

I enjoy being a coach. It warms my heart to help others grow. I was coaching before I knew what it was. In my corporate career I served as a consultant and coach. When I learned the difference, I leaned towards the latter. A consultant is a person hired to solve a problem. They come in, examine the situation, ask questions, and come up with solutions for you to choose that would be best for your company. They're the answer to your problem. A coach, on the other hand, works with you to come up with a solution together. They are not the answer. They take you through a series of questions and exercises so you can discover the answers yourself. Whatever the problem is, the coach's job is to make sure you have the tools to look inside yourself and tap into the resources already at hand. Your coach brings a spotlight to a dark place that holds the key to your solution for long-term effectiveness.

The coach is the lighthouse on a dark sea. When the fog comes in and you can't make out the markings to land correctly, the lighthouse shows you the way. It plays an essential part in the safe landing of a seafaring vessel. If you operate without one, you risk the danger of running aground and possibly causing short or permanent damage to your vessel. That can delay you or put you in danger, as well as your crew. My suggestion? Seek out the lighthouse. Though it's dark, your answer is in the light.

One more word of advice. We've been discussing doors and keys as being structures and materials. What you should also know is that you fall into that category as well. There's someone or something waiting for you to be the key to their

170

locked door, to their next level. The skillset you have serves as someone's doorway, threshold, partial door opening, automatic or solid door, or concierge service. The only limits you have on your life are the ones you put there. Remove the shackles from your mind and walk through the doorways of your life.

Acknowledgments

To THE ALMIGHTY: Thank you for life, health, and strength. Thank you for the gifts and talents you have given me that I may be able to help others manifest their dreams and visions.

To my wife, Nicole: I appreciate you more than you know. Thank you so much for the support throughout the years. I've talked about putting out books for years. Now, it's a reality. You have been such a wonderful help. This is just the start. I look forward to our new adventure as more is coming down the line. I love you!

To my Mom: Thank you for your support throughout the years. I appreciate you and love you! I marvel at your passion for family. I admire your constant sense of commitment and focus when it comes to helping others. You are truly our family Matriarch.

To my Mom and Pop in-love: I thank you for the calls, cards, and care that you have shown me from day one. I enjoy the times we spend together when we visit you. I truly value your presence, your advice, and your love.

To my coach Antoinette Harris: Thank you for the constant push and real talk I get from you on a regular basis. This book became a reality through your suggestions. I look forward to continuing to work with you and receiving your insight.

To my coach Chris Prouty: Your support and constant push has been a true blessing. I'm grateful for the favor and kindness you show me in pushing me to do my best with my businesses. The next steps in my businesses and the clients I work with will all feel the impact of my continued work with you. Thank you.

To my coach Gloria Jean Kelley: I thank you for being such a help and a voice in my life. Our coaching sessions are so full. I laugh, I learn, I gain more understanding. I appreciate the wisdom and the experience you pour out and am grateful for your insight.

To Andrea Susan Glass: Thank you for taking the time and effort to edit my book. I learned a lot from your years of experience and our many conversations. Thank you for the advice you gave and the continued encouragement.

To Victor Felix: My brother from another mother. Thank you for coming through in a clutch so many times. Thank you for the real conversations we have, for the constant encouragement, for believing in me. You are truly an inspiration and I appreciate you.

To Bishop John M. Borders III and First Lady Sandra Borders: Thank you, both, for your prayers and support. I have learned a great deal of watching you both lead, direct, comfort, and guide people in their time of need. Thank you for being a continual reservoir of kindness and caring.

To Archbishop Dr. Errol & Pastor Carol Estridge: Thank you for your continued prayers and encouragement. You have been such a great support throughout our marriage, checking in and being such beautiful examples for us to emulate.

To Archbishop Dr. E. Bernard Jordan and Pastor Debra Jordan: Thank you for the ministry that you have built over the last 40+ years. Thank you for leading from the future and creating platforms for so many people to grow, to develop, to find and mature their giftings. I appreciate the tools you provide, and the access granted to your knowledge, wisdom, and teachings.

About The Author

Born and raised in Boston, MA, Trevor Singleton (a/k/a Coach Trev, Your Accountability Coach) has been a fan of transformation and growth from a young age. His family will tell you that Trevor has always been drawn to music and the impact that it has on people and atmospheres, depending on the song that was played. One of the stories that they would always tell of him is how as a toddler, he would bang on his uncle's room door every time he heard music. Once he got there, he would just sit and listen.

As Trevor grew older, he began to see how words impacted people and their development. In school and in church, Trevor was involved with drama, recitals, and plays. He developed a deep understanding of tone and inflection. He saw how all these things play a part in creating an atmosphere and resonating with the audience. This would continue in his efforts in higher education, getting his Master's in Management with a concentration in Leadership and Organizational Development in Human Dynamics.

As Trevor progressed in his career, he was always drawn to positions involving training, development, coaching, management, and customer service. Trevor was really inspired when he can help improve their way of work or way of life. He would go to great lengths to help friends, family, co-workers, as well as senior level management. Eventually, he decided to widen his impact by starting his own coaching business (Single Source Coaching Solutions) and writing his first book, *The Doorways of Life*.

Trevor's goal is to help people to embrace transformative methods and ideas by discovering the talents that they have within, helping them to reach or exceed their expectation. Trevor has traveled to nearly all 50 states in the US as well as international locations to coach and consult clients. He enjoys working with people, helping them to awaken latent skills and use them to better those around them and their environment. Ready to put a smile on your face while keeping you on track, his tagline says it all.

"The foot in your backside
Making sure you don't backslide."

Contact & Social Media Info

Company Name: Single Source Coaching Solutions, LLC

Web: www.sscoachingsolutions.com

YouTube: Single Source Coaching Solutions

Facebook: Single Source Coaching Solutions

LinkedIn: SSCoachingSolutions

Instagram: @sscoachingsolutions

TikTok: @coachtrevsscs

Twitter: @CoachingSingle

Snapchat: trevor_wisdom

Made in United States
North Haven, CT
29 May 2023

37130948R00098